Ire

Garden Birds

A GUIDE TO ATTRACTING AND IDENTIFYING GARDEN BIRDS

Oran O'Sullivan is a wildlife writer and photographer based in County Wicklow. He worked at BirdWatch Ireland for 25 years and has watched birds for many more. He now works as an entrepreneur, promoting ways to inform and educate people to appreciate and recognise the wildlife in their back gardens and beyond.

You can track the movements and behaviour of garden wildlife on his blog and Facebook page, and visit the website and information hub at: www.irishgardenbirds.ie

Jim Wilson, from County Cork, is a wildlife writer, broadcaster and tour leader. A former chairman of BirdWatch Ireland, he set up the long-running BirdWatch Ireland Garden Bird Survey in 1987. His books include *Shorebirds of Ireland* (2009), *Freshwater Birds of Ireland* (2011) and *The Birds of Ireland: A Field Guide* (2013). He is also a regular contributor to *Mooney Goes Wild* on RTÉ Radio 1 and has played a key role in the national and international award-winning live annual broadcast of the Dawn Chorus from BirdWatch Ireland's Nature Reserve in Cuskinny, County Cork. Jim can be contacted at: info@irishwildlife.net

Ireland's Garden Birds

A GUIDE TO ATTRACTING AND IDENTIFYING GARDEN BIRDS

Oran O'Sullivan & Jim Wilson

The Collins Press

Bullfinch

Acknowledgements

A great debt of gratitude is owed by the authors to the photographers, especially Mark Carmody, whose work graces these pages. I would like to thank my former colleagues at BirdWatch Ireland for assistance, support and encouragement. A special thanks to all the garden bird surveyors who return survey data each winter to BirdWatch Ireland. Finally, to my family, Mairead, Dylan and Rhiannon, who put up with my regular window-gazing sessions when perhaps other urgent tasks beckon.
Oran O'Sullivan

I would like to thank the following for their invaluable support, help and advice in the writing of this book: Ann, Peter and Barry, Mark Carmody and Ciaran Cronin. Special thanks to designer Glen McArdle and to all the photographers who contributed to this guide, especially Mark Carmody who contributed all of the images to Part Two; and all those who watch and study birds, without whose knowledge this publication would not be possible.
Jim Wilson

Blue Tit

Part One

Introduction

Think of wild birds and, for many of us, wild places probably spring to mind: specialist habitats with specialist birds. Yet gardens are important wild-bird habitats and, more likely than not, the modern garden is in an urban or suburban location. There are over 2.2 million households on the island of Ireland and each year new developments are planned and completed. Whilst individual gardens are not attached to all dwellings (such as apartment blocks), it is acknowledged that green space comprises a conspicuous and significant portion of new housing developments. Older, mature and more expansive suburban residences built from the 1960s to the 2000s are likely to be even more important for wildlife, with their surrounding spaces and gradations of cover maturing and maintaining close links to the woodland model.

Relative to the built area, the garden portion of a residential property represents great value as a recreational living space. How you garden or 'decorate' this space is important: it will really affect conservation on a local scale and can potentially bring the countryside, the woodland and the meadow to your doorstep. Bearing in mind the constraints of your site, the plants you choose should reflect these natural habitats, many probably lost to make way for housing development.

Mixed borders are a delight for gardeners and wildlife alike

Whilst suburban spread has taken its toll on wildlife, it is, perhaps, ironic that some farmland species suffering declines in the country-side can and do thrive in domestic gardens. In addition, health profes-sionals are becoming increasingly aware of the benefits to people of watching birds at close quarters in urban and suburban environments. This access to nature has a positive effect on the quality of life for us all, both young and old. The educational aspect of garden birdwatching is

Great Tit

important, too: it is often the catalyst to an interest in bird conserva-tion and a wider support for the natural environment and awareness of issues such as climate change and sustainable living.

Although small urban gardens have been shown to attract fewer birds than large rural plots, the large number of the former garden type brings a relative importance to them and their effect on urban biodiversity.

As biodiversity plans roll out for larger urban areas, how we manage an increasing area of urban garden space is of paramount importance. Planning at a group or council level can deliver greater biodiversity. Thus a small garden can be linked in an interconnec-tion or corridor of garden spaces, with individual variation and retention where possible of mature features, thereby maximising urban diversity. Biodiversity is likely to be greatest when height, depth and variety, or complexity, of plants are present. However, height, depth and complexity only come with the passage of time in new gardens, though the choice of planting, garden management and design will ensure significant milestones along the way.

The management regime you implement as an individual gardener is likely to have a major effect on diversity even within your own garden space. Reduce the frequency of lawn cutting, allow variation of sward height and save on time and fuel. Allow and encourage the presence of naturally decaying plant material to support invertebrates. Cut back on use of limited resources such as water by planting drought-resistant varieties. Purchase a water butt to save free, soft rainwater. Seek alternatives to peat by producing your own garden compost. Avoid chemicals.

Finally, shorten your list of weeds or unwanted plants, and prac-tise tolerance. Make space and time to enjoy the fruits of your labour: the scents, sights and sounds of wildlife gardening are all around you.

Using this book

This book provides a general introduction to garden birds in Ireland. It also explains how gardens can be transformed into havens for birds and wildlife, giving practical advice on how to get the most from your garden, big or small, and describing the birds that you are most likely to see there.

Ireland's Garden Birds is written for people who enjoy garden birds but may know very little about them and would like to know more. Technical jargon is avoided wherever possible. Apart from one or two exceptions, scarce and rare birds are not dealt with. The book aims to be a continuing source of reference on our garden birds and, unlike many other guides, it deals solely with the garden birdlife of the island of Ireland.

The first section tells you all you need to know about gardening for birds, with practical advice on subjects ranging from planning your bird garden to a month-by-month bird garden diary. You will be given expert advice on what to grow and what to avoid. The second section describes the birds you are most likely to see in and around an Irish garden. Identification features, feeding suggestions, nesting information and interesting facts are provided for each bird species. This section also includes a photo gallery of all the species in the book, arranged so that similar-looking birds are shown side by side for quick reference.

Garden bird watching has brought us a lifetime of pleasure. Our hope is that *Ireland's Garden Birds* will start and sustain you on a similar journey.

Fieldfare

Gardening for Birds and Wildlife

What is a garden? Essentially, a garden is an enclosed area of ground associated with a dwelling house, with the primary functions of cultivation of plants for pleasure, food and shelter. A bird or wildlife garden extends these functions to cater for birds and wildlife, either as a priority or on a shared basis with the garden's other functions.

No matter what size your garden space may be, setting out a plan is time well spent. This might be achieved through a short set of objectives, a scale plan on squared paper or a plan worked from a software product.

Peacock butterfly on Verbena

Just as nature reserves are relatively small areas in the wider landscape, your garden plot is likely to be limited in space relative to the surrounding built environment. However, both examples set out to enhance their respective areas to the maximum for wildlife in general and, if managed correctly, become honeypots or special places for wildlife.

The chances are that both your garden and those of your neighbours replaced a farmed and hedged landscape, an area of woodland, a wet marsh, or a combination of all three. Plantings in such gardens will provide some mitigation for the initial loss of habitat. The sheer variety and number of even small gardens provide significant opportunities to create features of a woodland

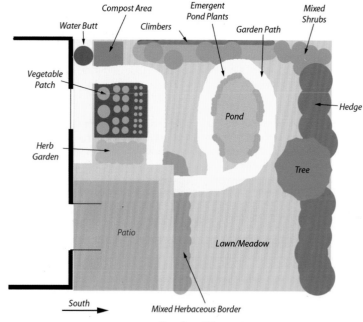

Compost Area
Water Butt
Climbers
Emergent Pond Plants
Garden Path
Mixed Shrubs

Vegetable Patch

Herb Garden

Pond

Hedge

Tree

Patio

Lawn/Meadow

South

Mixed Herbaceous Border

Garden Plan

edge, pond, meadow and tilled ground with composting facilities.

List the bird or wildlife habitats you want to create in your garden from the table below, being mindful of the restrictions of your site area, soil and orientation. A typical suburban garden might include:

- a lawn
- mixed borders featuring perennial plants
- mixed shrubs
- a tree
- climbers
- a hedge along a boundary
- a vegetable plot
- a pond
- a dry service area of gravel, patio or deck

To encourage wild birds and wildlife in general, provide at least two of the three principal objectives of food, water and shelter by choosing carefully from amongst these potential habitats.

Natives, Exotics and Invasive Plants

A garden should contain key native species, as well as a liberal selection of exotics such as the hardy perennials introduced from many parts of the world. There are good reasons for championing native plantings: a whole ecosystem or web of life has evolved around them and they are suited or adapted to our climatic conditions. An advantage of some exotics is that they have adapted to fit in with our climate and bring with them a myriad of additional planting and flowering opportunities to delight gardeners, birds and insects alike. As a general rule, many gardeners try to create a strong native framework (trees, ground flora, hedges and key shrubs), whilst celebrating summer with colourful exotic perennials and providing some special architecture plants to give shape and form throughout the year. Gardens are as prone to fashion trends as clothing, so try and

Pulmonaria

Japanese Knotweed

avoid too many quick-fit solutions, such as showy hard landscape features, painted surfaces and quick-cover hedging solutions, such as *Eucalyptus, Cypress, Griselinia,* etc.

Avoid exotics that are invasive: they have a tendency to jump the confines of a small space and spread beyond the garden without control, often outcompeting scarce native plants in fragile habitats on the coast or in the broader countryside and uplands.

Ⓝ Invasive land plants to avoid

Cotoneaster *C. microphyllus*	Seed spread by bird droppings to sensitive upland areas
Cotoneaster *C. simonsii*	Seed spread by bird droppings to sensitive upland areas
Himalayan Balsam	Self-seeds along watercourses, excluding native species
Hottentot Fig	Spreads along coast, threatening coastal plant communities
Japanese Knotweed	perennial capable of 2m of growth per stem annually

See www.invasivespeciesireland.com for a comprehensive list of unwanted plants and animals on the island of Ireland.

Garden Habitats

The Woodland Garden

Willow Warbler

Even a small garden or patio can accommodate a tree, for instance a cultivar such as weeping birch, a standard hawthorn, rowan or any one of a number of crab apples. Using the tree as a focal point, you can structure the areas under and around the tree by introducing traditional woodland species that will thrive in dappled shade, such as wild garlic, lungwort, violets, periwinkle, many bulb species and ivy. This ground-cover network provides interest throughout the seasons and in winter it insulates the ground from frost, allowing dunnocks and robins to forage through our hardest, shortest days. A medium or large garden will give you more options regarding the choice of tree and the opportunity to fill in the space from the ground to trees with a shrub layer (see table on p. 20 for options).

Herbaceous Borders

Hardy perennials in a mixed border offer some of the best value for gardeners and birds. They will grow best in a bed enriched with plenty of organic compost. The better the preparation, the better the results: perennials (having no woody stems or permanent structure) are long-lived and bring a world party to the garden planting: native origins are not an issue here! The foliage, as well as the flowers, supports a wide range of insects and provides microclimates for insects, birds and small mammals. If left to stand through autumn into late winter, the seed heads and decaying foliage of the herbaceous border will provide foraging and feeding opportunities for birds and insects. The herbaceous plants mix and match easily with small shrubs, alpines, grasses and bulbs.

Top 24 Herbaceous plants for any garden

shady: *Anemone, Aquilegia, Dicentera, Erythronium, Geranium, Hellebore, Pulmonaria, Trillium*

dry: *Berginea, Echinops, Echinacea, Kniphofia, Sedum, Stachys, Verbena*

damp: *Helenium, Astrantia, Astilbe, Euphorbia, Heuchera, Hosta, Achillea, Ligularia, Rudbeckia*

Hedges and Trees

A native hedge provides shelter and food and is much more interesting to wildlife (and the human eye) than a boundary fence or wall. Try to resist the temptation to plant easy-grow evergreen species such as *Griselinia* or *Leylandii;* native plants are far more valuable to birds and wildlife, and there are attractive options. Depending on your preference, the hedge could span both side boundaries or just the end boundary. An area 2–3m by 1m is required to allow growth sufficient to be of value, though pruning is necessary to keep shape and provide a strong, dense growth.

Herbaceous border

The best deciduous native is hawthorn, which, when established, provides fruit (or haws) in autumn and flowers in spring. With its thorny stems it is also stockproof, i.e. it will keep animals out and perhaps

Willow and Alder catkins

keep pets from straying, and can be purchased very cheaply as bare-rooted 'quicks' from nurseries in late winter for immediate planting. If evergreen cover is required, holly ticks the boxes for berries and stock-proof foliage. A mixture of the two, with one or two plants allowed to develop into small trees, will provide song posts for thrushes and perhaps nesting sites. A number of berry-bearing trees and shrubs (see table on p. 20) are suitable for inclusion in a mixed hedgerow.

Shrubs

If you are planting for wildlife, flowering and fruiting shrubs are a very important part of the planting scheme. A choice that encourages insect visitors is best. The amount of space you can provide will ultimately dictate your choice of plants; again, native berry-bearing shrubs are better for wildlife than some of the exotics, which are usually developed purely for gardeners' delight and show. However, there are non-natives such as dogwood (*Cornus*), coto-

Guelder Rose in September

neasters (*C. cornubia* is best) and *Pyracantha*, which serve birds and gardeners well. Most of the native planting options will require a space of 3–5m square for mature plants, but respond well to pruning. Even a small garden could accommodate a single specimen shrub or tree as a focal point. The best natives (for all-round interest and value) are hawthorn (as a standard tree or hedge), guelder rose (*Viburnum opulus*), spindle (*Euonymus europeaus*) and elder (*Sambucus nigra or S. racemosa*) if space is at a premium. All provide flowers for insects and good autumn leaf colour and berries for birds, and all favour dampish conditions. The table on the next page gives a summary of the relative importance of a number of shrubs for berry-eating birds (from 1 to 10, where 1 is the most important or preferential berry for each bird. Blank indicates that the berry is not used by the bird species).

Top Berry-Bearing Trees and Shrubs for Berry-Eating Birds*

	Blackbird	Song Thrush	Mistle Thrush	Fieldfare	Redwing	Robin	Blackcap	Starling
Holly	3	8	1	4	1		3	2
Yew	6	1	3		7	6		
Ivy	2	2	5	3	4	3	1	
Mistletoe			2					
Rose (hips)	4			2	9			
Hawthorn	1	5	4	1	2	9		5
Rowan	5		10				10	8
Whitebeam	9	10	6	8	3			
Cherry	7	9	9					7
Sloe	8	3	7	5	7	8		9
Blackberry						7		4
Crab apple				7				
Elder		4			1	2	2	3
Guelder rose		6						
Wayfaring tree						5	8	
Honeysuckle							5	10
Dogwood		7			6	4		1
Spindle				10		1	6	
Privet				9	8	10		
Buckthorn	10			8	6	5		6
Currant						9		
Nightshade						4		
Winter bryony						7		

* Adapted from *Birds and Berries* by B. & D. Snow

Herbs

With drier, warmer summers and milder winters, herbs from traditional Mediterranean countries are surviving Irish conditions, and if kept in pots, are movable. If a dry, sunny, gravel-based garden is to be planted, evergreen herbs are an ideal choice. Apart from their obvious usefulness as a culinary aid, herbs hold a great attraction for insects such as bumblebees, and attract them over a long flowering season. Herbs will flourish in a small sunny space from earthenware pots to patio fringe, or indeed a formal herb garden. Remember to keep them accessible to the kitchen!

Mixed herb garden

Top Herbs for Bees, Butter-flies, Hoverflies and Chefs
Angelica *Angelica archangelica*
Chives *Allium schoenoprasum*
Fennel *Foeniculum vulgare*
Lavender *Lavandula augustifolia*
Lavender cotton *Santolina sp*
Marjoram/Oregano *Origanum vulgare*
Mint *Mentha sp*
Rosemary *Rosmarinus officinalis*
Thyme *Thymus sp*

Mint

Climbers

Climbers are a space-saving group of plants that are ideal for the modern garden, providing vertical cover that will soften the harsh boundaries of a new plot. Ivy is a very important food source for nectar-seeking insects, and the late winter berries are available when most other food supplies have been exhausted. Just look at the table on p. 20 to see how attractive ivy's rich food source is to berry-eating birds, not to mention the possibilities for nesting birds. The anti-ivy lobby claims that it will bring down trees and walls if left unchecked. It can certainly hasten the demise of a diseased tree or unstable wall structure; however, it is not parasitic, its roots fend for themselves in the ground and the short 'roots' on climbing stems are for support only. Certainly, ivy needs space and is slow to flower until a significant area has been colonised and it reaches the top of its available support. The variety *H. arborescens* is slow-growing, but produces flowers and berries early on.

A seemingly endless range of decorative climbers such as clematis, honeysuckle, jasmine and potato plant all enrich the summer garden scene and are nectar providers for a wide range of insects in spring and summer. This range of plants requires partial or total support by way of a trellis or network of supporting wires. Most require sunshine for the showy foliage and shade or cool conditions for roots.

Lawns

The well-tended lawn is not nearly as popular as it once was in the gardening scheme of things: the advent of decks and hard landscaping has reduced the lawn area in gardens, and lawns are removed altogether where space and time spent on garden maintenance is at a premium. However, a lawn provides good feeding opportunities for a number of our most popular garden birds: robin, dunnock, blackbird and song thrush spring to mind.

Song Thrush in ivy

You can take steps to enrich the wildlife value of a lawn. The wildlife-friendly management of the lawn reduces the time spent on repetitive and boring maintenance. Resist the temptation to use fertilisers and weedkillers. Reduce time spent mowing by varying the height of grass throughout the plot. Short grass is good for hunting thrushes on the lookout for worms and other invertebrates. However, longer areas bear seed for sparrows and allow small insects a corridor and space between the flowerbeds and the shorter turf.

Meadow with Sika deer

Meadows

To take the wildlife-friendly lawn one step further you will most likely wish to consider a meadow scene interspersed with wild flowers. Assessment of soil type and the nature of the site to be planted will be paramount in selecting a suitable meadow mix. Specialist suppliers are able to assist once you have gathered this basic site knowledge. Meadows should have a closely mown path or network, for access and interest. Source an Irish meadow mix and avoid the danger of introducing non-native plants (see Website Resources, p. 194).

Vegetable Plot

In an age where calculating and reducing food miles (the distance food produce travels between grower and consumer) is becoming increasingly vital, you can take direct action and do yourself a favour into the bargain. The pleasure and satisfaction of growing a steady supply of fresh produce from your own plot is not to be underestimated. The time and space needed to produce a succession of fruit, vegetables and herbs can be reduced by choosing a range of key 'heavy croppers'. The other good news is that insectivorous birds such as robins

Vegetable plot

and dunnocks and many more will benefit from your digging and composting of the soil. Soil preparation and improvement with compost is the key to raising a successful vegetable crop.

Recommended for a Small Plot
Salad leaves, Fruit and Herbs
Green Oak Leaf Lettuce
Cocarde Lettuce
Mizuna
Sungold Cherry Tomato
Flat-leaf Parsley
Dill
Chervil
Vegetables
Blue Lake French beans
Painted Lady runner bean
Sytan carrot
Defender courgette
White Silver Swiss chard
Jersey Royal potato

Ponds and Damp Gardens

Ponds in an agricultural setting are largely a thing of the past, having been replaced by automated pumped watering systems and tanks. As a result, garden ponds have become increasingly important for the conservation of this valuable habitat.

In the wildlife garden, a pond introduces a distinct habitat complete with the highest diversity of invertebrates and the chance to plant a whole range of native plants grouped as 'submerged', 'floating' and 'emergent' (or edge) plants (see table, p. 26). This sequence continues to marginal bog- or damp-loving perennials.

The key to success is to create a shallow, irregular-shaped edge where invertebrates can emerge from dense wetland plants. A shallow, graded edge allows birds and small mammals a chance, literally, to walk in and dip their toes, drink and bathe.

A typical pond ecosystem should not include ornamental fish: they will decimate the tadpole population; even minnows and sticklebacks can pose a problem and are best not introduced. However, the pond is likely to be a very competitive and dynamic unit, with water beetles, pond snails, skaters and water boatmen representing the invertebrates, and frogs in all their various stages running the gauntlet of emergent dragonflies.

The design and size of the pond will be determined by your site, gardening requirements and other recreation priorities. (For safety reasons, families with toddlers may prefer to wait until the children are older before creating a garden pond.) A pond with a minimum area of 4m square is recommended if you wish to attract

Emperor dragonfly

dragonflies to feed and breed. They are voracious insect-eating carnivores and require a fair area to patrol. However, smaller damselflies and even dragonflies will visit a puddle to feed or drink. Remember, the bigger the pond site, the more soil to be distributed and disposed of! If possible, fill with rainwater from a water butt (see p. 28) rather than tap water.

Garden pond

Recommended Plants for your Pond*

Submerged

Spiked Water-milfoil
Myriophyllum spicatum

Whorled Water-milfoil
M. verticillatum

Curled Pondweed
Potamogeton crispus

Hornwort *Ceratophyllum Demersum*

Water starwort *Callitriche stagnalis*

Common spike-rush
Eleocharis palustris

Willow moss *Fontinalis antipyretica*

Marestail *Hippurus vulgaris*

Water Violet *Hottonia palustris*

Water Crowfoot *Ranunculus aquatilis*

See Website Resources, p. 195, for specialist advice

*Source: Royal Society for the Protection of Birds (RSPB)

Floating

White Water-lily *Nymphaea alba*

Ivy-leaved Duckweed *Lemna trisulca*

Frogbit *Hydrocharis morsus ranae*

Water Soldier *Stratiotes aloides*

Emergent

Yellow Iris *Iris pseudacorus*

Meadowsweet *Filipendula ulmaria*

Purple Loosestrife *Lythrum salicaria*

Rushes *Juncus spp*

Sedges *Carex spp*

Greater Spearwort
Ranunculus lingua

Water Mint *Mentha aquatica*

Water Forget-me-not
Myosotis scorpioides

Frogs

The pond site should include sun and shade. A pre-formed rigid pond liner will last longer than a PVC or rubber butyl liner. However, the PVC option is likely to give more flexibility for wildlife, being easier to manipulate to create shallow, wavy edges. Ponds will be colonised naturally, but plants from neighbours or friends are welcome, provided you exclude alien weeds. Remember, it is illegal to remove plants and other pond material from the wild.

Ⓘ Alien Pond Plants to Avoid

Invasive plants prove to be extremely problematic and, when introduced to waterways, spread easily, choking ponds and outcompeting native plants. Once established, they are very difficult to eradicate. Avoid plants from the following list when considering a pond or bog area:*

Australian Swamp Stonecrop/ New Zealand Pigmyweed *Crassula helmsii*

Parrot's Feather *Myriophyllum aquaticum*

Floating Pennywort *Hydrocotyle ranunculoides*

Japanese Knotweed *Fallopia japonica*

Water ferns *Azolla filiculoides and a. caroliniana*

Indian/Himalayan *Balsam impatiens glandulifera*

Water Lettuce *Pistia stratiotes*

Giant Salvinia *Salvinia molesta*

Water Hyacinth *Eichornia crassipes*

Water Chestnut *Trapa natans*

Canadian Waterweed *Elodea cnadensis*

Nuttall's Waterweed *Elodea nuttallii*

Curly Waterweed *Lagarosiphon major*

*Sourced from Plantlife and RSPB

Composting

Composting is the most natural thing in the world. Convert the waste materials from your kitchen and garden into a free source of organic matter for reuse in the garden. Then look at the big picture and see what 'refuse' you have diverted away from landfill, a genuine win–win situation for wildlife gardeners! Local authorities provide custom-designed composting bins made from recycled plastic materials at subsidised prices.

Compost bin

It's All in the Mix:

Kitchen and garden waste breaks down rapidly in warm summer months.

Dry, woody materials are very slow to break down and are best layered and watered.

Damp grass clippings break down rapidly but will form a slimy mass if over-provisioned; combine with dry matter.

Turning a half-filled bin provides air to the heap.

Cover the heap to retain heat.

Worms and other small creatures aid the recycling process, but keep cooked food out of the process to discourage rodents.

Water Butts

Collecting rainwater is a useful water-conservation measure. Soft and without lime, not only will it be appreciated by acid-loving garden plants, but it is the natural and best way to top up garden ponds. A rain or water butt should be attached to a downpipe via a diverter. You can make your own from an old barrel with a lid: site it slightly raised from the ground to allow for fitting a tap. For a variety of reasons, it makes good sense to purchase water-saving devices such as plastic water butts that easily divert rainwater from your gutters and downpipes. Some local councils now supply a recycled plastic butt with fittings at a subsidised price.

Water butt

Bird Gardener's Year Planner

	J	F	M	A	M	J	J	A	S	O	N	D
Plant trees & shrubs	✓	✓	✓								✓	✓
Prune trees & shrubs	✓	✓									✓	✓
Start landscape projects	✓	✓	✓									
Take hardwood cuttings	✓											
Put up nest boxes	✓	✓							✓	✓	✓	✓
Feed birds	✓	✓	✓	✓	✓	✓	✓	✓	✓	✓	✓	✓
Spread mulch & apply compost		✓	✓	✓	✓	✓						
Check ponds for ice	✓	✓	✓									
Plant perennials		✓	✓	✓	✓				✓	✓	✓	
Plant summer bulbs			✓	✓								
Sow hardy annuals					✓							
Sow vegetable crops				✓	✓	✓	✓	✓	✓			
Mow lawns				✓	✓							
Trim meadows					✓							
Prune early flowering shrubs & heathers				✓						✓	✓	
Plant spring bulbs										✓	✓	✓
Deadhead perennials						✓	✓	✓				
Rake lawns/harvest hay							✓					
Take cuttings							✓					
Trim evergreen hedges							✓	✓				
Transplant shrubs & evergreens								✓	✓	✓		
Final cut meadow							✓					
Plant winter salads							✓					
Sow cabbage & broccoli							✓					
Plant bare-rooted hedges & trees									✓	✓		
Clean out & repair nest boxes									✓	✓		
Prune roses									✓			
Dig vegetable patch & borders										✓	✓	✓
Prune fruit tees & bushes											✓	✓
Collect compostables & leaves											✓	✓
Transplant tender plants											✓	✓
Plan beds & borders										✓	✓	✓

The Bird Gardener's Year

January

Birds

The garden plants may be sleeping, but the birds will never be more active; the shortest days of the year coupled with some of the coolest temperatures and the gradual exhaustion of natural food supplies brings a real urgency to feeding for survival. All of this means that your feeding station will really hum with activity. Harsh weather conditions in northern Europe will often be reflected in a rise in garden bird numbers: blackcaps readily feed on windfall apples and peanuts; starlings that may breed in Russia will arrive in the garden to probe a lawn and mop

Blackcaps

up kitchen scraps. Winter thrushes, i.e. redwing and fieldfare from Iceland and Scandinavia, will come in from the fields to take any remaining berries.

It may seem strange that birdsong begins to feature in the winter garden. Mistle thrushes deliver their plaintive refrain from an aerial or tree, marking out their territory, often through inclement conditions: not surprising then they are known locally as 'the storm-cock'. The same species will jealously guard the fruit crop of rowan or holly on their territory, busily and noisily chasing away all comers.

Gardens

New Year is a new beginning and the time to put a few resolutions to the test. This is perhaps the last opportunity to put up a nest box or two, or clean out existing ones. Hedge pruning and trimming should be carried out now, before the nesting season. Resist the temptation to tidy up remnants of last season's flowering perennials; seeds and cover are valuable for foraging wrens and dunnocks that have a specialist diet largely unenhanced by food from the bird table. Enjoy the first bulbs of the new year, such as aconites and snowdrops, and keep an eye on outdoor pots which are prone to cracking during frosty spells. Winter Jasmine and Witch Hazel provide floral interest.

February

Birds

The bird feeders continue to be at their busiest. It is important to provide continuity and keep feeders well topped up. Siskins often make a sudden and welcome appearance; they are quite nomadic and ringing recoveries bear witness to their wanderings around Ireland and the UK, largely in response to exhausted food supplies in forests and woodlands.

A rare exotic nomad that visits gardens in search of berries and fruit is the waxwing. They erupt in some years out of Scandinavian forests in late autumn, spreading south and west through the winter months. This movement is in response to a crash of the rowan berry crop in the north, coupled with high population levels following a successful breeding season. Waxwings often form flocks in urban locations, literally clearing city parks of rowan and cotoneaster berries.

Gardens

Ground-cover plants show encouraging signs under trees, with lungwort *(Pulmonaria)* showing unique pink and purple flowers, all set off by spotted foliage. Other natives such as ramsons break through the ground and the green foliage provides a contrast to the flowering primulas, cyclamen and celandines. Woody plants such as dogwood and birch brighten the scene with bright bark features. It is a good time to prune dogwood in particular. The

Blackthorn

attractive bright red or green bark is borne on fresh growth only. In the south, blackthorn hedges are resplendent with white flowers.

March

Birds

At last, longer days are here, and with them a chorus of birdsong that increases in variety and intensity: expect to count up to ten species making themselves known vocally. Song flights and threat displays are becoming more commonplace as the life focus moves from mere survival to breeding. Blackbirds often show the earliest signs of nesting, with beak-loads of mud and grass. You can help nest-builders by gathering moss, twigs and grasses into habitat or debris heaps. Males deliver their measured, tuneful song on still evenings. The blackcaps that winter often reveal themselves by their scratchy songs before they head back to central Europe to breed. Incoming summer migrants to your area may include sand martins and chiffchaffs, two of the earliest arrivals to our shores.

Gardens

Hedges are putting on green foliage, spring bulbs are vying with each other and the woodland floor or shady garden is lively with wood avens and lungwort.

Weather conditions are typically mixed through the month (or the day, in some cases), but nevertheless hawthorn hedges are greening up and daffodils, crocuses and muscari are in full bloom. Mixed borders receive a new lease of life, and periwinkle and heathers are in full flower, providing nectar for bumblebees and small tortoiseshell butter-flies.

April

Birds

The nesting season for our resident species is in full swing and foraging insect-eaters are attracted to lawns and well-mulched borders. Keep seed and peanut feeders well stocked and they will continue to attract finches and later-nesting tit species. By providing protein-rich foods at this time you will

Starling in ivy

ensure that the birds are in good condition for the challenges of the nesting season. The first spring migrants will make themselves known by their distinctive songs: chiffchaffs that have arrived earlier continue to sing, while the similarly plumaged willow warblers are distinctly different in song and in their choice of damp willow scrub. Swallows and martins make their way back to traditional nest sites, though it will be May before the full complement is evident.

Gardens

The tidy-up after winter takes on an even greater urgency; this is important in borders where perennial weeds should be removed before consolidating and seeding. Remove dead stems on perennials to allow fresh growth through and remove debris from the edges and floor of ponds. Good nectar suppliers at this time include hellebores and fritillaries, which bring great interest to borders. *Dicentra* ('gentlemen's breeches'), Comfrey, star of Bethlehem, alpines such as *Aubretia*, *Arabis* and *Alyssum* are at their peak and enliven a cast that is expanding with extra daylight for plants and gardeners. Vegetable plots are ready for a great variety of spring seedlings and early March sowings will have germinated, along with a complement of weeds that need to be removed to the compost heap.

After all this activity, you might wish to just sit back, relax and enjoy the bright and sudden appearance of cherry blossom, a feature of suburban drives and many gardens.

May

Birds

With a full complement of spring migrants and the first young broods of robins, starlings and blackbirds fledging, the garden will never seem busier. Keep a sharp eye out for one of our scarcer and more subtle summer visitors, the spotted flycatcher. They are late arrivals and will favour larger, more mature gardens with leafy mature trees such as ash providing lookout points from which to hunt insects, and walls covered with

Spotted Flycatcher

creepers, providing ideal nest sites. Although their subtle plumage and call notes may mean that some escape detection, they seem to be genuinely thin on the ground.

Swifts, house martins and swallows become evident around urban and rural homesteads. The focus both for garden birds and arriving summer migrants is towards protein-rich insect prey for young birds in the nest. Wet weather can spoil this party, however, and a successful breeding season for many garden birds depends on a cycle of events in nature that match the hatching of hungry broods of young birds.

Gardens

With frosts ruled out in most cases, the wildlife garden becomes a cornucopia of growth and diversity. Early summer can be either bone dry, or wet and windy or something in between. Remember to water pot and container plants if necessary. It is time to cut back some of the early bloomers: alpines, early bulbs and *Clematis* that have completed flowering, but check for nests and nesting activity first! With all this fresh growth, it's time to step up late evening garden patrols to remove slugs organically: no need for bright blue chemical solutions when beer dregs in a sunken cup or just sheer presence on the beat can readily provide the same result. You could also use copper tape around pot plants or broken seashells and sharp grit to cordon off an area.

Bee in Geranium

June

Birds

How quickly the spring passes! Some birds have completed their breeding cycle, though blackbirds and thrushes, collared doves and woodpigeons raise or attempt to raise many broods into June and beyond. Family parties roam gardens; the tit family in particular emit lots of calls and sub-calls on the wing and the youngsters are still begging to be fed. The later summer migrants are only now beginning to hatch young: house martins, swifts and spotted flycatchers in particular are high-season breeders. Look out for the juveniles: drab robins, dusky dunnocks, and tailless pied wagtails, to mention a few. The first fledged swallow broods are to be seen lining up on electricity wires.

Gardens
Providing food for birds is now less important, as most young birds benefit from the natural and high-protein crop of insect prey in the garden. We advise you to stop providing dry bread and whole peanuts: both can be fatal for young birds. By allowing the birds to utilise insect prey such as aphids and caterpillars (instead of using insect sprays) you are on the road to organic and sustainable gardening and doing the birds a favour too.

Early spring-flowering shrubs can be pruned now and if your lawn is more like a meadow, cut now. Annuals can safely be potted up in containers and the more tender vegetable crops can be sown directly outdoors. Potted plants in particular may require watering: think about using plants that need less watering and are more suited to a drier climate, such as lavenders and other herbs.

July

Birds
Hazy days of summer, but where are the birds? They tend to go quiet at this time, without need for song, as territory no longer requires defence or advertisement. After the rigours of the breeding and nesting season, adult birds enter a period of moult, dropping whole tracts of worn feathers to replace them with a new suit for the winter ahead. During this phase birds are more at risk to predators, being partially flightless, so they are less likely to show themselves around the garden but will benefit

House Sparrow

from shrub cover around the garden plot. Early autumn parties of bright yellow juvenile willow warblers can make an appearance in the garden, a post-breeding dispersal that leads to full migration south to Africa. They are attracted to aphids on trees in full leaf, such as birch and willow. Bullfinches and siskins can reappear at this time, feeding on the ripening catkins of silver birch.

Gardens

Water, or lack of it, can be a problem in high summer: many people have been adapting their plantings to a less dependable climate by adding specialist dry Mediterranean plants in dry, gravel gardens. Now is a good time to plant up container-grown plants in a prepared bed. Providing water for birds is likely to be very important this month, both for bathing and drinking. You can conserve or save rainwater by siting a water butt (see p. 28) under a shed or house eaves to catch run-off.

August

Birds

One of our latest arrivals, the swift, is already departing for Africa: their shrill screams and evening gatherings, typically in an urban setting, are to be treasured now, as departure is often sudden. Birds that have completed their autumn moult, such as robins, make a welcome reappearance. Indeed, robins are likely to burst into territorial song in this month as the population adjusts its boundaries amidst brief flurries around the garden. Look out for final broods of song thrushes and blackbirds; the latter often choose to roll sideways to catch the rays and sunbathe in sunny corners.

Blackbird sunning itself

Goldenrod

Gardens

Some perennials are coming into their own just now and *Asters, Echinops,*

Goldenrod, Gelenium and *Penstemon* provide lots of autumn interest. Many others will need dead-heading and evergreen hedges can be trimmed back now. Ornamental grasses show nice seed heads, and seeding vegetables can also provide an autumn food source for birds.

September

Birds

Broods of summer visitors such as swallows and house martins gather in increasing numbers on roadside wires and hunt for insects high into the late summer sky. Some adults may be involved in fledging a final late brood, often very successfully as insect food can be plentiful at this time.

Silver-washed Fritillary

Gardens

Seed heads of biennials and annuals such as sunflower and teasel should be saved for their seeds, to be put out in winter for the winter bird visitors. Some prolific berry-bearing native shrubs will be set upon by garden birds: black elderberries and the bright red berries of guelder rose will be well patronised by thrushes, sparrows and tits, all taking advantage of the early autumn fruit crop. Rowan berries have a habit of vanishing quickly, though seem to last longer in urban areas.

Red Admiral on Teasel

October

Redwing

Birds

The first of the winter visitors to Ireland can be heard at night: the thin calls of redwings are often noted on cool, still nights, en route from Scandinavia. They are unlikely to feature in gardens until much later in the winter, preferring to forage in fields and hedgerows. Other migrants that will pass through gardens at this time are goldcrests and starlings.

Gardens

Enjoy the colours of flowering perennials such as *Penstemon*, Michaelmas daisies and anemones. Foliage colours are also very interesting right now as frosts trigger a palette of gold amongst a host of interesting shrubs and trees. October is a good month to dig new beds for perennials or vegetables.

November

Birds

With shorter days and cooler temperatures, flocks of finches and tits begin to build around the bird feeders. This month sees the start of BirdWatch Ireland's annual Garden Bird Survey, which runs through to February and is a valuable yet simple monitoring tool for garden birds. To get involved, check out their website. You can expect anything from 20 to 40 species over the course of the winter, so keep the feeders stocked and sit back and enjoy.

Gardens

November is a good time to plant bare-rooted native hedges, shrubs and trees, all at a fraction of the price of container-grown plants. Invest in the future now: plant spring bulbs for a succession of spring colour, gather leaves for leaf mould, and put up a nest box now in readiness for spring. Resist over-tidiness: seed heads are useful to birds and small mammals over the lean winter months.

Birdfeeder

December

Birds

Robins face the winter with brave song, to defend and mark out a territory in advance of the breeding season. Others such as the blackcap will defend a 'territory' around a feeder, chasing away sparrows, tits and finches. This aggression has helped them survive a winter that was more usually spent around the Mediterranean and West Africa. No doubt provision of windfall apples and peanuts has helped, though blackcaps are particularly fond of seed bracts on cordylines, as well as ivy berries.

Robin in winter

Gardens

Divide perennials now, and prune fruit trees and shrubs. Protect climbers and young trees by ensuring that support stakes are sound. Plan for the new year.

Feeding and Caring for Garden Birds

Autumn and Winter

After the quiet late-summer period, you may begin to notice that bird populations are at their highest, with juveniles abounding, before inevitable winter mortality weeds out weaker individuals. Once fruiting shrubs and trees are depleted and temperatures drop, small birds will seek out protein-rich food from your feeders.

If you are feeding birds, regularity is the key. Try to keep your feeders well topped up, and if you have kitchen scraps, put them out first thing in the morning. Thoughtful commuters who rarely see their gardens in the dark months of winter often use extra-large feeders, capable of taking up to 2kg of peanuts, to cover the whole of the working week. The colder the weather, the more birds and feeding activity there will be to witness. Put out food and water on a regular basis. Birds require high-energy fatty foods during the coldest weather, when fat reserves are necessary to survive the long winter nights.

Spring and Summer

Jay

You can continue to feed birds with seeds and peanuts into mid-spring and summer, once supplied in the correct feeders and not spread loosely. However, even seed-eating birds such as sparrows and finches will move to insect prey to feed their young. Not surprisingly, specialist bird food suppliers can supply mixes containing insects and fruits for feeding at this time. Many bird watchers choose to scale down the feeding regime some-what in the summer months (May to July), but correctly dispensed and appropriate foods will be appreciated by many garden birds, as the stresses of rearing young and a late-summer moult of body feathers weaken adult birds. You should avoid using loose peanuts or peanuts in lightweight mesh feeders that can be tampered with by crows and squirrels. Peanuts and dry bread fed whole to nestlings are likely to swell up in the gizzard and choke youngsters.

Hygiene around the bird table and feeders is very important and needs to be considered. (see p. 50).

Feeders

There is an ever-increasing range of specialist feeders to store and dispense bird food.

Siskins on a Nyjer seed feeder

Tables: The most common basic feeder is a roofed table, sited on a pole or slung from a tree. This provides shelter from rain and predators and also allows access for all but the largest opportunistic species. Choose a table with a roof not more than 14cm from the table to exclude crows and gulls. Food scattered from the table to the ground is usually cleaned up by the shyer ground-feeding species. However, if you are providing nuts and seeds, as distinct from kitchen scraps, you will need to dispense the food in an appropriate feeder to maximise value for the target group of species. These feeders can be suspended from branches or bird tables, put on top of a pole or swung from window brackets.

General seed feeders: clear plastic cylinders with a number of feeding ports for on-site feeding by tits, finches and sparrows, amongst others. These are suitable for sunflower seed, sunflower hearts and mixed seed. Try to put seed feeders in a dry, sheltered spot because wet seed swells and rots quickly.

Nut feeders: Wire, mesh-clad and designed to hold a stock of whole shelled peanuts to be chipped away at by finches and tits. Peanuts rot quickly at the end of mesh feeders, but removing the plastic ends and sealing the mesh, by pinching and folding the bottom, stops the rot and allows the feeders to be cleaned more easily.

Nyjer feeder: Ultra-fine seed such as Nyjer seed, originally from Ethiopia, requires its own container; a plastic cylinder with the tiniest of slits (or ports) that retain the fine seeds but allow them to be delicately removed by siskins, redpolls and goldfinches.

Window feeders: Nearly any of the above feeders can be hung on a specially designed suction bracket, guaranteed to bring close-up views of some of the bolder species, such as robins and great tits.

All the above feeders come in a range of sizes and qualities from light plastic to heavier metal-trimmed versions designed to withstand 'attacks' by squirrels and crow species. The bigger the feeder, the less refilling required, which can be useful for commuters out of the house for extended periods. But remember, if the peanuts are not being eaten at a reasonable rate they will dry out and rot.

Food to put out for Garden Birds

Small birds in particular spend up to 85 per cent of short winter daylight hours feeding, just to survive. Any fat reserves built up during the day are used up overnight when birds roost in cold conditions.

A seed mix containing sunflower seed

Bird-seed mixtures are pre-packed mixes that vary in quality and variety. Check the contents for seeds such as sunflower, maize, oats and millet, all attractive to smaller birds. Wheat and barley grains are really only suitable for ground-feeding pigeons, doves and pheasants and are a cheap 'filler'. Dried peas, rice and lentils are not edible to smaller birds and should be avoided. In general, the more specialist foods are more expensive but provide the highest calorific values and cut down on 'mess' or waste, an important factor in many small gardens where non-target species are not to be encouraged.

Woodpecker feeding on peanuts

Black sunflower seeds are a very popular food, particularly with coal tits who regularly visit seed feeders and take away seeds to store in a food cache. The oil content is higher in black sunflower seeds than in striped ones.

Sunflower hearts are seed hearts, minus the hard outer shell or husk of the black sunflower, allowing a variety of species easier access and feeding efficiency to a high-energy food, which is important, particularly in hard weather when there are fewer daylight hours for foraging.

Nyjer seeds have very high oil content. Because they are so small, you will need a special type of seed feeder with minuscule feeding ports. The seed is a particular favourite of goldfinches, siskins and redpolls, which have the long, fine beaks capable of dealing with this food.

Peanuts are rich in fat and are popular with most garden birds, right up to rooks and jays. They originate in far-flung places such as India, West Africa, Argentina and China. The premium qualities are tested and passed for human consumption. They are best provided in metal feeders where the nut is gnawed at rather than taken away whole. Fallen debris below feeders is popular with collared doves, dunnocks and robins. Salted or dry-roasted peanuts should never be used. Peanuts can be high in a natural toxin (Aflatoxin), which can kill birds, so buy fresh, dry stock regularly, to minimise the risk to birds from poisoning (See troubleshooting p. 49).

Fat Balls and bird cake: Pre-mixed balls, squares or cylinders of fat mixed with a variety of seeds are popular 'treats' and can also be made up to your own recipe. Children will enjoy the 'cooking' process and be enthralled by the antics of tits if you place the food ball on a window feeder. It is not recommended to purchase food or fat balls in light plastic mesh; if you do, please remove the mesh, as birds' toes and feet can become trapped in it. Small food balls, without the mesh, can be dropped one at a time into a peanut feeder or impaled on a thorny shrub. Food candles and pellets come with their own hanger or feeder and are recommended.

Bird-Cake Recipe
Pour melted fat (suet or lard) onto a seed mixture and include any of the following ingredients: nuts, seed, dried fruit, oatmeal, cheese and cake. Use about one-third fat to two-thirds dry ingredients. Stir well in a bowl and allow the mixture to set in a container of your choice. Refrigerate to harden. An empty coconut shell or plastic yoghurt pot hung upside down with string makes an ideal bird-cake feeder. Alternatively, just place it on the bird table.

Kitchen Scraps for Birds

Birds will be attracted to most cooked scraps from the kitchen. Bear in mind the scraps may also attract the larger, more boisterous species. Cooked food might also attract rodents, which are likely to be even more unwelcome. Only put out enough food to be eaten in, say, 30 minutes or less, and don't put out kitchen scraps late in the day, but hold them over for an early-morning feed.

Favourite Bird Foods for Ireland's Top 20 Garden Birds

	peanuts	mixed seed	bird cake	sunflower hearts	black sunflower seeds	Nyjer seed	kitchen/bird table scraps
Robin	✓	✓	✓	✓		✓	✓
Blackbird		✓	✓	✓			✓
Blue Tit	✓	✓	✓	✓	✓		✓
Chaffinch	✓	✓	✓	✓	✓	✓	✓
Great Tit	✓	✓	✓	✓	✓		✓
Greenfinch	✓	✓	✓	✓	✓		✓
Magpie	✓	✓	✓	✓			✓
Coal Tit	✓	✓	✓	✓	✓		✓
Wren			✓	✓			✓
Goldfinch	✓	✓	✓	✓	✓	✓	
House Sparrow	✓	✓	✓	✓	✓	✓	✓
Dunnock		✓	✓	✓			✓
Song Thrush			✓	✓			
Starling	✓	✓	✓	✓			✓
Siskin	✓	✓	✓	✓	✓	✓	
Jackdaw	✓	✓	✓	✓			✓
Collared Dove		✓					
Woodpigeon		✓					
Rook	✓	✓	✓	✓			✓
Blackcap	✓		✓	✓			✓

Nest Boxes

There is a certain pride, not to mention fascination, in having birds nesting around your garden. There is also the added bonus that the young are all fed on insects, many of which are pests in the fruit and vegetable garden. If you have a choice, put up nest boxes in the autumn or late winter. Birds may well use the box over the winter months to roost and will prospect the box in spring. The siting of the box is very important, and will vary depending on the type of box (open-fronted or hole-fronted) and species targeted. The box shouldn't expose the intended occupants to predators or to the elements.

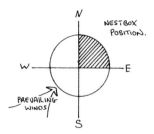

face the nest box between north and east, to avoid direct sunlight

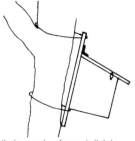

tilt the nest box forward slightly

Seek a place that will provide natural shade for the box during the day, and ideally face it between north and east, to avoid strong sunlight and prevailing winds and rain. Tilt the box slightly forward so that any driving rain will hit the roof and bounce clear. Remember, nest boxes bring you closer to garden birds and their daily trials and tribulations: mortality of eggs, chicks and adult birds can result in a sorry end to a nesting season. Birds lay big clutches and repeat clutches to cater for these eventualities. Don't be disappointed if birds

Open-fronted nest box

do not use your nest box in the first or even second year. It can take a few years for them to use it and sometimes moving it to a different location might be needed as there might be something wrong with the original location that you did not notice. Always remember that the birds know best and don't read the books!

Specialist boxes for popular summer migrants such as house martins and swallows are increasingly important where modern living excludes old outbuildings with suitable openings, and fosters intolerance to 'untidiness' around the house and garden. House martins will use a cup-shaped nest box with a crescent opening, placed under eaves or a gable end. Placing a 15cm-wide shelf about 1m below the nest will catch most droppings if they become a problem. Swallows use an open-topped cup nest box, placed in a porch or shed, with access through an open window or gap. For specialist boxes mentioned in the species accounts we recommend consulting the BirdWatch Ireland website and shop or consulting a specialist DIY guide such as Nestboxes, by Chris de Feu (see Bibliography, p. 193).

Top Ten Users of Garden Nest Boxes

	hole-fronted box	open-fronted box	preferred height
	hole diameter	front opening	
Blue Tit	25mm	–	>2m
Great Tit	28mm	–	>2m
House Sparrow	32mm	–	>2m
Robin	–	60mm	<2m
Pied/Grey Wagtail	–	60mm	2–4m
Wren	25mm	60mm	< 2m
Coal Tit	25mm	–	<2m
Starling	45mm	–	>4m
Spotted Flycatcher	–	60mm	>4m

Hole-fronted box

Open-fronted box

Fixing and Maintaining Nest Boxes

You can make or buy a nest box. If buying, choose a nest box from a supplier or manufacturer that places substance over style. Wooden boxes can be treated with a water-based preservative that will not affect the birds. Fixing your nest box to a tree with nails may result in damage to the tree. It is better to attach it either with a nylon bolt or with wire covered in a length of hosepipe around the trunk or branch, or to use a screw that can be loosened off.

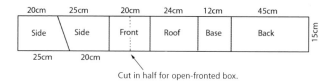

20cm	25cm	20cm	24cm	12cm	45cm	
Side	Side	Front	Roof	Base	Back	15cm
25cm	20cm					

Cut in half for open-fronted box.

Nest box plan using approximately 15mm thick timber or exterior plywood

There should be a hinged panel giving access either from above or the side to allow for cleaning and nest removal after the breeding season (September or October). Various feather parasites and insect scavengers may be present, and some will disperse in the initial cleanup. Boiling water will kill off parasites; let the box dry out thoroughly before replacing the lid. Don't use insecticides or flea powders!

The box can be enhanced as a winter-roosting place for small mammals or birds by scattering hay or wood shavings into it once it has dried out after cleaning. Remember: this can deter birds from using it for nesting unless it is removed in late winter.

Boxes for Biodiversity

There is such a range of boxes for just about every garden creature – bats, bees, bugs, hedgehogs, frogs, etc. – to the extent that some commentators have grown cynical and question how

Hinged lid on a House Sparrow nest box

wildlife survived before the advent of the wooden box. However, don't let this attitude discourage you: natural hole sites are in short supply. Well-sited boxes set in a good garden design and planting will ensure a healthy stream of visitors to the garden.

Birdbaths

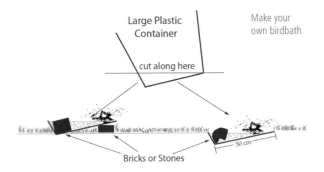

Large Plastic Container

Make your own birdbath

cut along here

Bricks or Stones

50 cm

Water is very important for birds, especially during the winter. A small birdbath will attract a surprisingly large range of birds. If you are not keen on putting out food in a wildlife-friendly garden, a birdbath can provide an alternative source of entertainment, with birds of all shapes and sizes coming to drink and wash. Water can be put out in a wide variety of containers, but all should be shallow, with gently sloping sides for easy access for birds of all sizes and should not be more than 10cm at the deepest. Anything from an upturned plastic bin lid to a garden pond will do the job. You can buy an ornamental birdbath on a stand. Make sure it fits the criteria above. Alternatively, you can put one on or in the ground. You can make one with cement or use an old dustbin lid or plastic container. If the bottom of a broken plastic dustbin or a large plastic container (minimum 50cm diameter) is removed, this will also make a fine birdbath (see illustration above). When cutting the end off the dustbin, or any other plastic container, do not cut it straight across but rather at an angle, thus providing a sloping bottom to allow birds to wade in to whatever depth suits them best. Dig a shallow hole in the garden to accommodate the birdbath. If you don't want to make it a permanent feature, just lie it on the ground, put a stone or brick under the shallow end and put another stone or brick in the deep end of the birdbath to stop it from being blown away in a gust of wind. Put the birdbath in the open, like the bird table, to avoid ambushes by cats. Most importantly, put it somewhere you can see the birdbath action from inside your house. Replace the water regularly, especially if it starts looking murky or if the container becomes filled with leaves. In frosty weather, break the ice if you have a pond, or empty and refill the birdbath early in the morning. Do not use hot or warm water as this may kill the birds quicker than the cold.

Troubleshooting

(Sorry, you're not invited)!

If you set out to attract birds and animals to your garden, don't be surprised if a few species crop up that are stronger and bossier and may become a nuisance. If you don't like uninvited guests, you can minimise the effect of boisterous invaders through careful husbandry. The grey squirrel is a non-native mammalian example; birds such as magpies and feral pigeons attract a similar bad press. However, there is less sympathy for the owner of a backyard feeding station, 'plagued by a flock of noisy house sparrows, not to mention rough starlings and pigeons …' You might not realise that the starlings and sparrows are considered to be threatened species in Ireland and Europe – many gardens have none. There are specialist products and attachments such as squirrel- or crow-proof cages that help eliminate or reduce the use of feeders by larger non-target species.

An unwelcome visitor at a bird table

The success of a bird-feeding regime is also likely to be noticed by predators such as the sparrowhawk, which will hunt along garden boundaries and know when to patrol and stoop on the active wildlife garden. BirdWatch Ireland maintains that feeding small birds does not increase the predation of songbirds by sparrowhawks – it only makes it more obvious to many by bringing both kinds of bird closer to view. In any event, the presence of a predator such as the sparrowhawk indicates a healthy garden bird population.

Many will argue that cats are a greater threat and are a numerous and generally unwelcome visitor to most gardens. Unlike birds of prey, cats are not natural garden-bird predators. Hunting by cats is not necessary for their survival, and most are well looked after by conscientious owners. Their habit of catching birds and bringing them to the doorstep is particularly galling during the breeding season (or any time of year!). Deterrents are available: use one or, even better, two bells on cats' collars. Sonic deterrents are also available. Keep cats in overnight if at all possible and let them out in the morning after the birds' busy dawn-feeding period. If you are not a cat owner, but are visited by neighbours' cats, you can discourage them by use of deterrents, such as pepper, coffee grounds or a commercial repellent.

Hygiene in the Garden

With sensible precautions and some common sense, you should be able to maintain a safe and clean environment for birds, animals and humans.

- Regularly move feeders around the garden.
- If you are concerned about possible disease or hygiene issues, don't feed in warm summer months.
- Use gloves when handling bird feeders and/or wash hands thoroughly after refilling and washing feeders.
- Regularly scrub birdbaths, bird tables and feeders or any feeding area, using 10 per cent disinfectant solution. Rinse out several times after treatment to ensure all traces of the chemical have been removed. There is a range of cleaning products available from specialist suppliers.
- Water containers should be rinsed out daily during the summer months and fresh water added.

Disease Amongst Garden Birds

Drowsy, fluffed-up greenfinches hanging around bird feeders are an indication of salmonella infection. This infection is transmitted by droppings from an infected bird. A number of other diseases, such as trichomoniasis, a parasite that affects the throat of species such as greenfinches and house sparrows and which results in starvation, and *E. coli,* etc., can appear from time to

Removing an old nest

time. Once birds are visibly sick, it is rarely possible to treat them successfully. If you suspect an outbreak of disease or infection, it is usually best either to suspend feeding altogether or clean and move feeders to a fresh location in the garden after a rest period.

While the incidence of picking up an infection from birds in your garden is very rare, it is always best to take precautions, since there is the potential for some diseases of wild animals to be transmitted to people. Always take extra hygiene precautions if you have any contact with infected birds, feeders or droppings.

Avian Influenza and Garden Birds

Both BirdLife International and its partner, BirdWatch Ireland, have published very useful information and guidelines about garden birds; check their websites and the Department of Agriculture and Food website for further information.

Almost everybody at some time or another comes across a bird that looks abandoned or injured. Most people are afraid to go near the bird and don't know what to do with it. Birds are delicate creatures and, in most cases, if injured or sick, cannot be rehabilitated, even in the hands of the specialist. In many cases, simply attempting to handle a sick or injured bird may result in additional trauma to the bird.

Dealing with Sick and Injured Birds

Some garden birds will pick up disease and infection. We would not recommend that you handle any bird that looks sick, as there may be a risk of it transmitting a viral or bacterial infection.

If you feel you must handle or move an injured bird, take strict hygiene precautions. Wear gloves, because the bird might cut you with an infected beak or foot. Always wash and disinfect your hands and clothing properly afterwards.

If the bird is caught in something like old string, try to cut the bird out rather than untangling it, which can do more harm than good.

Remember, birds that appear very badly injured can still be very lively, so don't put your face too close to them as they might strike out and injure you. Be especially careful with long-necked

'Leave me alone'

and sharp-beaked species such as herons. Trying to pick up a bird of prey such as a hawk or owl can be very dangerous. Their talons are lightning fast and razor sharp. Thick leather gloves are essential.

If necessary, transport the bird in a ventilated box. If it is not en route to a vet or animal welfare shelter, keep it in a draught-free, dark and quiet place. Do not put it too near a direct heat source such as a fire or radiator. Birds that are stunned from striking a window will often recover if left in a safe, stress-free environment. At first they may not be able to stand or sit and may look almost dead, but after a few hours they can make an astonishing recovery. Do not be tempted to check on the bird too frequently. This could finish off an already distressed bird. If the bird has improved but still looks unable to fly, leave it overnight and check it first thing the next morning. If it still looks unwell, seek specialist help for its treatment.

Young Birds

If you find a young bird, the best advice is to leave it alone. All young birds eventually get too big for the nest and have to move out. They will stay on a branch or on the ground, not far from the nest, and wait for the parents to return to feed them. They may look as if they are in trouble but are almost always quite all right. Ducks and pheasants have young that leave the nest soon after hatching, relying on the camouflage of their down and feathers to hide them until their parents return with food. If the bird is in obvious danger on a busy footpath or near an entrance to the house, etc., move it as short a distance as possible to safety and wash and disinfect your hands afterwards. Resist the temptation to bring it inside. The parents will find it when it calls for food. Even if the bird looks orphaned, it is best to leave it where it is and return for a look the following day. If it still looks in trouble, watch it from a distance for at least an hour to be sure the parents are not feeding it. Only then consider bringing it into care. Your first port of call should be your local vet. A call to your local centre of the ISPCA or RSPCA may be worthwhile. Non-governmental organisations such as BirdWatch Ireland and the RSPB are not animal-welfare organisations and do not have facilities for the care and rehabilitation of young, sick or injured birds. However, their websites offer practical advice.

Ringed or Tagged Birds

Occasionally you might come across a bird in your garden with a small metal ring on one of its legs. If the bird is dead or injured, or caught in something, you may be able to get a close look at it. You will notice words and numbers inscribed on the ring. For very small garden birds, such as the goldcrest, a magnifying glass may be needed to read this information. The ring will have been put on the bird by a highly skilled bird ringer in order to learn more about our garden birds. Ornithologists all over Europe have been studying birds in this way for over a century.

These studies are very important if we are to learn about birds' needs and to give us an early warning if their populations are in trouble. The ring does not hurt the bird and is extremely light. If you manage to see one of these rings and want to help in these important studies, write down the following information: the metal ring number (double-checking that you have written it down correctly, as the number may be very long, and if the incorrect number is submitted all your efforts and those of the ornithologists will be for nothing); the address

A swallow being removed from a mist net

Metal ring on a bird's leg

on the ring; the full address of where the bird was found; when it was found; and if the bird was dead or released alive. You can then submit your information to the British Trust for Ornithology either online at www.bto.org or by post to: BTO, The Nunnery, Thetford, Norfolk IP24 2PU, England. If the bird is alive, be very careful not to damage its leg while reading the ring. Do not attempt to remove the ring and once you have all the information written down release the bird as soon as possible. Racing pigeons have closed, coloured plastic rings; for further information on what to do if you find one that is exhausted or injured go to the Irish Homing Union website at: www.irishhomingunion.com

Watching and Recording your Observations: The Garden Bird Survey

We have a proud tradition of watching, feeding and recording numbers of birds in our gardens. However, gardens are generally not well studied in terms of their general diversity, certainly not in proportion to their importance in the urban environment. BirdWatch Ireland's Garden Bird Survey runs every winter, over a 13-week period from the very end of November to the end of February. The survey involves anything from 700 to over 1,600 gardens making annual returns from all around Ireland. A grand total of over 110 species have been recorded in Irish gardens, with 65 per cent of gardens hosting up to 25 species. Large rural gardens attract the highest numbers of species, though suburban gardens compare very favourably and are by far the most popular and widespread garden type.

Typical survey results show that a small number of gardens record between 30 and 37 species, all of which have been rural in type. However, the next closest gardens were suburban gardens in the east of the country, hosting a very respectable 30 species. Overall, half the gardens participating are suburban and only 5 per cent of gardens are classified as urban.

If you would like to take part in this survey you can download survey forms or enter your observations online at: www.birdwatchireland.ie

Top of the Tree

Ireland's favourite garden bird, the robin, is firmly established on top, retaining number one position as the most widespread species and present in virtually all Irish gardens. Other highlights in the top ten include the continued rise of goldfinches in the ratings and conversely, the fall of greenfinches, thought to be a reflection of their susceptibility to the trichomoniasis disease.

Ireland's favourite bird – the Robin

Winter Warblers

Irish gardens are increasingly important to one species of warbler, the blackcap, though chiffchaffs have also been recorded, albeit in much smaller numbers and in only 2 per cent of gardens. The lesser whitethroat, the other warbler recorded in winter gardens, is far rarer still and is a very rare winter visitor to Ireland. The blackcap occurs in nearly 50 per cent of our winter gardens and its position in the Garden Bird Survey hovers within the top-20 mark.

Survival of the Fittest

Blackcaps are particularly interesting due to the fact that a central European population has in recent decades begun to use a winter survival strategy that increases its chances of breeding success. We know from ringing studies that Ireland's breeding blackcaps winter from south-west Europe southwards into West Africa. These birds depart our shores from September through October. The Garden Bird Survey has shown blackcaps present in

Female Blackcap

small numbers in November, doubling by Christmas and remaining constant until the survey ends. Indeed, the wintering birds often break into snatches of song in February and March. The wintering birds in Irish gardens are from a breeding population originating in central Europe that formerly wintered in Iberia and North Africa. On the back of warmer winter temperatures, coupled with bird-friendly gardens and a shorter migration commute to winter in Ireland, these blackcaps return to their breeding grounds earlier than the southern wintering population, and not surprisingly claim the best breeding territories, increasing their breeding success and increasing the genetic tendency in the local population to migrate to Ireland.

Wintering blackcaps will take a variety of ornamental berries, are particularly fond of ivy berries, a great late-winter standby, and also congregate around showy *Cordyline* trees, feeding on bracts of berries. They are known to be highly territorial, chasing tits from peanut and fat feeders, and are fond of apples, cut in half and speared on branches. Wintering blackcaps are more likely to be seen in suburban gardens in the east and south of the country, where conditions suit these birds that are literally on the edge of their winter range.

Finches at the Feeders

The chaffinch has traditionally occupied the top spot amongst this colourful group of birds, which depend on seed to carry them over the winter months. They have only once moved outside the top five in recent years. The chaffinch flocks may vary in number, reflecting the milder conditions and consequent reduction in need for northern European populations of this species (often females only) to migrate down the fringes of the North Sea and English Channel into Ireland for the winter. Goldfinches are the real talking point amongst garden-bird enthusiasts. This is not surprising, as they are extremely showy, with perhaps the most striking plumage mix of any garden bird coupled with a pleasant call and song and often very animated presence around the feeders.

Their remarkable success is well documented by the Garden Bird Survey, showing that fewer than 15 per cent of gardens hosted goldfinches in 1995, compared to 85 per cent of gardens in 2015, showing a dramatic shift in ranking from 25th to ninth in that period.

Ireland's Top 30 Garden Birds in Winter 2012/13 compared to 2002/03

	% of gardens	2012–2013	2002–2003
Robin	99	1	2
Blackbird	99	2	1
Blue Tit	98	3	3
Great Tit	96	4	7
Chaffinch	95	5	4
Coal Tit	94	6	8
Magpie	91	7	5
Goldfinch	85	8	13
House Sparrow	82	9	12
Greenfinch	81	10	6
Dunnock	79	11	11
Wren	78	12	10
Starling	77	13	15
Song Thrush	72	14	9
Woodpigeon	71	15	18
Jackdaw	70	16	14
Collared Dove	67	17	19
Siskin	65	18	17
Rook	64	19	16
Hooded Crow	53	20	25
Blackcap	49	21	20

Pied Wagtail	49	22	21
Long-tailed Tit	47	23	22
Bullfinch	43	24	24
Redpoll	42	25	27
Mistle Thrush	28	26	26
Goldcrest	26	27	23
Feral Pigeon	26	28	31
Sparrowhawk	17	29	28
Pheasant	13	30	32

The siskin is a small finch with a characteristic feeding position: this is usually upside down on nut feeders. Its position over the years has ebbed and flowed from 15th to 29th. This fluctuation most likely reflects the availability of its natural forest food: conifer seeds and seed of alder and birch. Siskins are highly mobile, particularly in late winter when ringing studies have confirmed journeys around Britain and Ireland over a short period. They are most likely to appear in gardens in late winter or early spring, and their appearance in gardens can coincide with rain: wet conditions close the seed cones of their favourite spruce trees.

Siskin

The 'forgotten' finch is probably the bullfinch, the male glaringly bright in breeding plumage, but generally quiet around the garden where its subtle though characteristic mewing call struggles to draw attention. They now visit feeders and are attracted by sunflower hearts in particular.

Bullfinch

We have seen bullfinches utilise birch seed and rowan berries in autumn and hawthorn berries and buds in late winter, all with great gusto, with food remains sticking to its pug face. They will also take a wide selection of weed seeds in season .

Bullies and Thieves?

Some people who feed garden birds are concerned that the smaller birds are affected by the presence of predators such as the sparrowhawk and crows in general, with the magpie being considered public enemy number one. This is despite the fact that numerous studies have concluded that there is no correlation between magpie numbers and a decline in songbird populations.

Magpies fighting

Magpies are present in 91 per cent of Irish gardens, the seventh most widespread species; they are most abundant in suburban gardens, particularly in the east of the country. The colourful jay is one species of crow that is rather shy and retiring in its garden visits; however, it has recently taken to peanut feeders and it now occurs in 10 per cent of Irish gardens. Its population has benefited from the afforestation of our countryside and is a clear demonstration of the link between woodland birds and gardens.

Scandinavian visitors

Redwings and fieldfares are welcome additions to the winter garden scene. They breed in Scandinavia (redwings also breed in Iceland) and migrate south in winter, typically foraging over open farmland with traditional hedgerows, such as hawthorn and holly, which are a source of berries. In late winter they often move south and west to avoid hard frosty weather and will also visit urban and suburban gardens and parks to avail of remaining berry stocks of rowan and *Cotoneaster*. Rowan berries seem to last longer in built-up areas, there being less 'demand' from resident species, a fact often affecting distribution of another occasional winter visitor, the waxwing. Waxwings are often referred to as 'an irruptive species', arriving in numbers in some winters and absent in others. Their movements are determined by availability of rowan berries in their northern homes, with a berry failure resulting in a mass exodus south and west in autumn/winter. They frequently occur around supermarket car parks as well as gardens, where ornamental berry bushes have been planted. They can often be seen sitting up on electricity lines, starling-like, as they digest the strong seeds and juice of winter berries. Their direct and swooping flight, together with their size and structure, also recalls the starling. They have a distinctive jingling call often delivered in flight, a handy aid to their identification. Once located in their favourite berry bushes, they are at once very distinctive and exotic looking.

Happy Garden Bird Watching!

We hope you will be encouraged to feed your garden birds by carefully selecting planting schemes to provide natural foods or by providing supplementary food, or better still a mixture of both. Our garden birds will reward you with hours of fascinating close-ups of wildlife in action, right outside your window.

Waxwings

PART TWO

Identifying Ireland's Garden Birds
Getting Started

The notebook

Apart from this guide, the most important book when watching garden birds is your notebook. This is used to write down what you have seen, where and when you saw it, and anything you feel is important to keep as a record. It is also used to take descriptions of birds you cannot readily identify. Without your notebook, by the time you get out this guide the bird may well have flown away, never to be seen again. You won't be able to remember details, blue may become green, grey may turn to black, streaking disappears, and size and shape become distorted beyond belief. You may end up convincing yourself that the bird you spotted is the same as the first bird you come across in the book which looks vaguely like it, passing over 'minor' details such as its extreme rarity in your part of the island or the fact that there are very similar species which are far more common than the one you've picked!

With a little practice, you can record a large amount of information about a bird in a short space of time by using drawings or sketches. You do not need a degree in art. In fact, you do not need to be able to draw well at all. Most people can draw better than they imagine. If you wanted to give someone directions you would preferably draw a map rather than have them remember details in their head. When identifying birds it is the same thing – think of your humble sketch as a map rather than a work of art.

What to Look at When Taking Notes

Size

Birds are rarely found on their own. There are nearly always other birds close by. If there is a bird you know nearby, compare it with your mystery bird and note down its size, i.e. smaller than a robin or the same size as a woodpigeon. Try to do this without looking through binoculars or telescopes as these can sometimes distort size.

Shape

When identifying a bird, judging its shape is very important. The essential parts of a bird to look at are the beak, legs, wings and tail. Is the beak thin like a blue tit's or thick like a greenfinch's? Are the

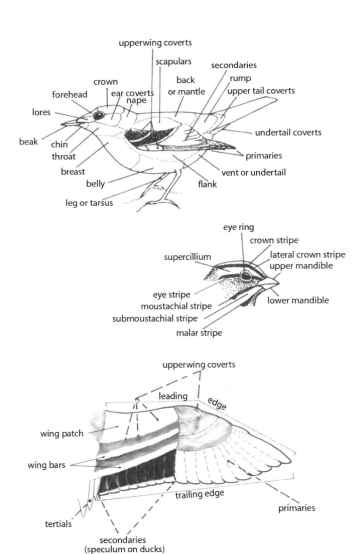

upperwing coverts
scapulars
secondaries
crown
back
rump
forehead
ear coverts
or mantle
upper tail coverts
nape
lores
undertail coverts
beak
chin
primaries
throat
breast
vent or undertail
belly
flank
leg or tarsus

eye ring
crown stripe
supercillium
lateral crown stripe
upper mandible
eye stripe
moustachial stripe
lower mandible
submoustachial stripe
malar stripe

upperwing coverts
leading
edge
wing patch
wing bars
trailing edge
primaries
tertials
secondaries
(speculum on ducks)

Bird Topography

Bill shapes: 1. insect eater; 2. seed eater; 3. meat eater; 4. fish eater

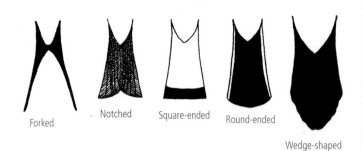

Forked   Notched   Square-ended   Round-ended

Wedge-shaped

Tail shapes

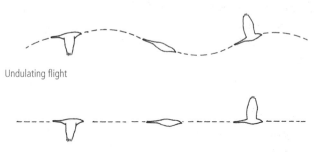

Undulating flight

Straight flight

legs short or long, thin or fat? Are the wings long and narrow like a swift's or broad and short like a pheasant's?

Is the tail relatively long like a magpie's or short like a blue tit's? It is also very useful to note the shape of the end of a bird's tail – is it square, rounded, wedge-shaped, notched or forked?

Patterns

The variety of patterns, stripes, lines, patches, bars, spots, etc., on birds is almost infinite. Recording the most striking patterns is important. Firstly, note the wing patterns. Are there any patches or wing bars? Is the tail all one colour? Look carefully: many birds, such as finches and buntings, have pale outer tail feathers. The tails of young gulls might have a dark band on the end. The bird's back might be plain or striped, sometimes very subtly. The underside might be plain, streaked, spotted, or a combination of all three. Head patterns on birds can be very complex. The rook has a plain head pattern but the blue tit has a very complicated one. Record any features that stand out and try to get to know the different parts of a bird by studying the illustrations in this book on pp. 61 and 62. Don't worry if you can remember only some of the parts. Your knowledge will improve with practice.

Colour

One area of bird identification that can cause great difficulty is the description of the colours of birds. For instance, rooks are not actually black but a beautiful dark iridescent blue. Light conditions and wear of the feathers alter colour. Whether the feathers are wet or dry will also affect their colour. All these things must be borne in mind when describing the colours on your mystery bird. Try to refer to colours of birds you already know, for example 'robin' red, 'blue tit' blue, etc. It is not always enough to say that the bird was brown. You should always try to be more exact. For instance, it might have been grey-brown, which means that it was mainly brown with a hint of grey, or red-brown, which is also mainly brown but with a hint of red. Both of these colours are brown, but look completely different from each other. Some birds can be leucistic, or albino, making part or all of the bird's plumage white or washed-out looking, most noticeably on birds with dark plumage. These white feathers can make it hard to identify a bird that would otherwise be easy to categorise. Finally, don't forget to record the colour of the bird's legs, beak and eyes, but beware: wet or dry mud or earth on beak and/or legs will often hide the real colour.

Call and Song

Bird calls and songs have been the inspiration for many poets, such as Shakespeare, Thomas Hardy and Austin Clarke, and composers such as Mahler, Sibelius, Ravel, and many traditional Irish musicians. But, try as they may, even these experts of sound have struggled in vain to record accurately what birds really sound like. What is the difference between a call and a song? A call is usually very short and not at all musical. It is the sound a bird makes when it wants to tell others of its own kind where it is or when it is alarmed for some reason. An example is the call of finches as the flock flies over a field, or that of long-tailed tits moving along a hedgerow. This keeps the flock together and raises the alarm for other members of the flock when one senses danger is near. The song, however, is usually very musical and is used primarily to tell other birds of its own kind to keep out of its territory, and also to attract a mate. As a general rule, the duller the colour of the bird the more musical is its song.

Recording the sounds of your mystery bird can help identify it. Most mobile phones have a sound-recording option or there are free apps to download that will do the job. If you do not have a sound recorder handy, write down what your mystery bird sounds like. A song 'graph' might help, to show where the notes went up or down and where there were pauses between notes. People have used words and phrases to remind them of a bird's song. For example a yellowhammer 'says' something like '*a little bit of bread and no cheese*'. Separating the calls of the collared dove and woodpigeon is easy if you remember that collared doves seem to 'say', '*Can yoouuu coo ... can yoouuu coo ...*', while the similar-sounding woodpigeon 'says', '*take two, John, take two*'.

Habits and Habitats

Finally, it is important to note what the bird was doing and where it was seen as well as its physical description. Was it wagging its tail all the time? Was it always on the ground or in bushes? Was its flight fast and straight like a wren's or undulating like a finch's? Did it fly close to the ground or high in the air? Was its stance upright or almost horizontal? Did it stay out in the open or did it hide deep in a bush most of the time? Was it calling all the time? Was it singing out in the open or out of sight? Bear in mind where your garden is situated. Gardens near the sea may get seagulls while a garden in or near woodlands might have a better chance of getting jays.

All of these observations are very important because, while there are exceptions to every rule, bird species generally have habits peculiar to themselves and tend to prefer certain habitats. Learning to record what you see and hear will improve with practice. The value of your records will also increase with time, both personally and as part of BirdWatch Ireland's Garden Bird Survey if you decide to get involved. By doing so, you will help monitor the fortunes of birds and support their conservation. Check out their website for more information on this fun survey.

Species Profiles

Explanation of the Key

Bird species are arranged here in taxonomic or scientific order, in two-page spreads. Fifty-seven species have been chosen: there is a good chance of seeing 30 species in an Irish garden over a few years. Arrows indicate the key features to look at in order to identify the species or tell the sex or age of the bird. **Note: the images on the plates are not drawn to scale.**

Key to abbreviations on the species plates

Br. – Breeding plumage
NBr. – Non-breeding plumage
Ad. – Adult
M. – Male
F. – Female
Eclipse plumage – some male birds, especially the ducks, have plumages they acquire for a short time after breeding through what is called a post-breeding moult. This plumage is called 'eclipse plumage' and can make males appear very similar to the female of the species.
Juv. – distinctive juvenile plumage shortly after fledging.
Im. – plumage of immature birds not yet in full adult plumage but which cannot be aged with confidence. Gulls and some other species will be in immature plumage (Im.) for up to four years. More specifically, such species can be aged as follows: **1st W.** – 1st winter, **1st S.** – 1st summer, etc. This language describes a plumage associated with a bird of a particular age, before reaching adult plumage, i.e. 1st winter would be a bird in its first winter after hatching; 1st summer is the first full summer after hatching. **2nd Yr.** – 2nd year is a bird in its second calendar year after hatching.

Species Name: This is given in English, followed by the Latin name. Some local name(s), where known, are also given, followed by the name in Irish.

When to See: This quick-reference guide shows you which months of the year you are most likely to see the species

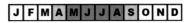

Example: swallow a summer vistor

in your garden. Dark green indicates 'best chance to see in and around gardens'; yellow indicates 'possible chance to see'; and white indicates 'little or no chance to see'.

The feeder icon indicates the bird's ranking in BirdWatch Ireland's annual Garden Bird Survey, carried out each year between November and February by over 800 of its members. The bird ranked number 1 is the species seen in most gardens.

 For summer visitors, the summer icon indicates the percentage of BirdWatch Ireland's Countryside Bird Survey squares in which the species was recorded nationally (in the period April to June).

Length: is expressed in centimetres and represents a measurement of the bird from the tip of the beak to the middle of the end of the tail. You can get a good impression of relative measurements by comparing sizes of two common birds such as robin and blue tit.

Wingspan: is given in centimetres and represents a measurement of the bird from wing tip to wing tip.

All-Ireland population/wintering population: A population estimate is given for all breeding species. Those that winter here only are similarly estimated where data is available. The figures quoted are best estimates based on data from Olivia Crowe *et al: Generating population estimates for common and widespread breeding birds in Ireland* (Bird Study 2014), previous bird atlases, and more recent Irish opinion estimates and from European status guides published by BirdLife International.

Identification Features: This section together with the voice guide is highlighted in a pale blue box at the start of each species account and describes the main identification features of each species.

Voice Guide: The song and call of each species is given. Phonetic translation is included to give the reader a general idea of what type of sound the bird makes. It is intended that the phonetic translation will point the reader in the right direction rather than provide a definitive translation. Listening frequently to the songs and calls of birds you have identified is the best way of improving your bird-sound identification skills. www.xeno-canto.org is an excellent online bird-sound recording resource.

Diet: describes the food that each species usually eats in the wild.

Food to put out: indicates, where appropriate, what food can be put out to attract the species being described into your garden. Where peanuts are mentioned, we mean peanuts in hanging mesh feeders.

Nesting season: when the birds are most likely to be nesting and rearing young.

Nest location: where the nest is usually built.

Nest: what the nest looks like.

Eggs: are described as follows: normal number of eggs laid, the average length of the egg in millimetres, and a description of the egg's appearance. Because of the huge variation that can occur in colour and pattern, the description is only to be used as a very general guide.

Incubation period: the length of time the birds will incubate or sit on the eggs before they hatch. Many species start incubating the eggs only after the last egg is laid, though some species, particularly birds of prey, will start before that. For most garden-nesting birds the female usually carries out most if not all the incubation duties and the male feeds her during the period.

Fledging time: the number of days the young will remain in the nest and/or depend on the parents for food after hatching until they are able to fly and fend for themselves.

Number of broods reared per year: the number of clutches or families usually reared annually.

Nest box: information on whether the species will use a nest box or not and if so, what type, as discussed in the nest box section on p. 45.

Average lifespan: lifespan information comes from the analysis of bird-ringing data collected over many years by the British Trust for Ornithology (BTO) which manages ringing data from Ireland also. For some species the average lifespan is unknown because there is insufficient data.

Oldest known individual: This information also comes from analysing ringing data collected over many years by the BTO.

General Information: provides the reader with interesting additional information on each species.

Confusion Species: indicates, where appropriate, other species that may be confused with the species being described. Only key differences are described and reference is made to the page where a full species account can be found.

Note: images not to scale

Mistle Thrush p. 132

Song Thrush p. 128

Redwing p. 130

Fieldfare p. 126

Meadow Pipit p. 108

Spotted Flycatcher p. 142

Pied Wagtail p. 112

Grey Wagtail p. 110

Starling p. 164

Swift p. 100

Rook p. 160

Jackdaw p. 158

Hooded Crow p. 162

Blackbird (F.) p. 124

Blackbird (m.) p. 124

Great Spotted Woodpecker p. 102

Magpie p. 156

Note: images
not to scale

House Sparrow
p. 166

Tree Sparrow
p. 168

Chaffinch (F.) p. 170

House Sparrow (F.)
p. 166

Wren p. 116

Dunnock
p. 118

Robin (Juv.)
p. 120

Stonechat (F.)
p. 122

Redpoll
p. 182

Linnet (M.)
p. 180

Coal Tit   p. 146

Long-tailed Tit
p. 144

Great Tit
p. 150

Blue Tit
p. 148

Yellowhammer (M.)
p. 186

Greenfinch (M.)   p. 174

Siskin (M.)
p. 178

Siskin (F.)   p. 178

Note: images not to scale

Brambling (M.)
p. 172

Chaffinch (M.)   p. 170

Goldfinch
p. 176

Yellowhammer (F.)
p. 186

Reed Bunting (M.)
p. 188

Reed Bunting (F.)
p. 188

Jay
p. 154

Waxwing   p. 114

Blackcap (M.)   p. 134

F.

Bullfinch (F.)
p. 184

Treecreeper
p. 152

Goldcrest   p. 140

Willow Warbler
p. 138

Bullfinch (M.)
p. 184

Chiffchaff
p. 136

Robin   p. 120

Stonechat (m.)   p. 122

Swallow p. 104

House Martin
p. 106

Kestrel p. 84

Barn Owl p. 96

Long-eared Owl
p. 98

Sparrowhawk
p. 82

Herring Gull
p. 88

Black-headed
Gull p. 86

*Note: images
not to scale*

Pheasant (M.)
p. 78

Pheasant (F.) p. 78

Mallard (F.) p. 76

Mallard (M.) p. 76

Grey Heron
p. 80

Woodpigeon
p. 92

Collared Dove p. 94

Feral Pigeon p. 90

Feral Pigeon p. 90

Mallard *Anas platyrhynchos*

Lacha fhiáin

J F M A M J J A S O N D

Length = 58–62cm
Wingspan = 81–98cm
All-Ireland population: 23,000 breeding pairs

Rank
50
Garden Bird Survey

Seen in
<1%
of gardens in Ireland

Identification features

Male: iridescent blue-green head; thin white neck ring; yellow-green beak and unusual up-curled feathers at base of whitish tail. **Female:** dull brown; identical in shape to the male; beak reddish-orange with variable amounts of dark brown; lacks curled tail feathers. When moulting, mainly in July, males resemble females except for the yellow-green beak. **In fight:** white-bordered blue-purple speculum on both male and female. Flies straight with rapid wing beats.

Voice guide: The female makes a wide variety of calls ranging from the classic *quack* to a call that sounds as if it was laughing at you. The male makes a much quieter *wheep* sound.

Diet: wide range of aquatic insects and aquatic vegetation. Where people regularly feed ducks and swans with bread, they will also eat that.
Food to put out: Lettuce or cabbage leaves and seeds on the ground.
Nesting season: March to May.
Nest location: will nest in a variety of locations, usually on the ground, in wetland areas under bushes and in undergrowth but will sometimes nest on buildings in urban areas.
Nest: a hollow in the vegetation lined with a mixture of plant material, down and feathers. Eggs are covered with down when the female is away from the nest. Built by twhe female.
Eggs: 10–12, 57mm, unmarked eggs ranging in colour from almost white to pale green, blue or light brown.
Incubation period: 28 days by the female.
Fledging time: Young leave the nest and feed themselves soon after hatching. They remain with the female for some time and can fly after about 55 days.
Number of broods reared per year: one.
Nest box: hole-entrance nest box.
Average lifespan: three years.
Oldest known individual: 20 years.

eclipse M.

ducklings

F.

M.

F.

Confusion species

Males are unmistakable; females can resemble females of other duck species.

General information

The original ancestor of most domestic ducks, the mallard is our most common surface-feeding duck. About the size of a hen, the mallard can be found almost anywhere in Ireland where there is water, from estuaries to rivers and lakes, and parks in the middle of towns and cities. Young birds can dive, especially when frightened. Often interbreeds with domestic ducks, especially in towns and cities, resulting in the most bizarre-looking offspring and an identification nightmare for the beginner. Irish mallard rarely travel very far but are joined in the winter by mallard from Iceland and Scandinavia. The plain brown colour of the female is so different from the male that they were originally thought to be separate species.

Pheasant *Phasianus colchicus*

Coilleach coille

Length = 71–89cm
Wingspan = 70–90cm
All-Ireland population: 300,000 individuals

Rank
30
Garden
Bird Survey

Seen in
13%
of gardens
in Ireland

Identification features

Male: unmistakable red face, white neck ring on most individuals; plump body; short legs; tail longer than its body. **Female:** mottled brown, shorter tail. A fast runner and usually flies only when absolutely necessary. **In flight:** rapid wing beats interspersed with glides, rarely travels more than a 100m before diving for cover.

Voice guide: The best time of year to hear a pheasant is in late spring or early summer when the male 'sings', making a loud hoarse sound like a loud rusty gate.

Diet: Feeds on the ground and will often dig up roots. Has a varied diet of seeds, vegetable matter, insects, spiders, etc.

Food to put out: seeds and bread on the ground.

Nesting Season: mid-April to mid-June.

Nest location: Nests on the ground in a wide variety of habitats from farmland to bogs.

Nest: a small hollow in the ground, usually unlined.

Eggs: nine to 13, 46mm, shiny unmarked eggs, colours varying from pale brown to olive or blue-grey.

Incubation period: 25 days by female only.

Fledging time: 12–14 days; young leave the nest soon after hatching and can feed themselves but stay close to the female for some time.

Number of broods reared per year: one.

Nest box: no.

Average lifespan: no data.

Oldest known individual: no data.

Confusion species

Female or young pheasants are often mistaken for corncrakes, which are an extremely rare summer visitor and secretive; short tail, half the size; rusty-brown wings and a rasping *crex-crex* call.

F.

M.

General information

A very distinctive game bird, often seen foraging along roads or exploding from cover along the margins of farmland. Believed to have been introduced into Ireland around 1590, probably from Britain or Western Europe, but originating in the Caucasus in Eastern Europe where pheasants lack a white neck ring, and later China where they have a white neck ring.

Found in good numbers everywhere in Ireland except west Mayo and parts of the north. The 'wild' population is supplemented by the release of hand-reared birds by gun clubs and up to 200,000 are shot each year. BirdWatch Ireland's Countryside Bird Survey indicates a slight decline in recent years.

Grey Heron *Ardea cinerea*

Crane   Corr éisc/Corr réisc   **J F M A M J J A S O N D**

Length = 90–96cm
Wingspan = 150–173cm
All-Ireland population: 3,650
breeding pairs

Rank
47
Garden
Bird Survey

Seen in
3%
of gardens
in Ireland

Identification features

Adult: large dagger-shaped beak; white head, with a thick black stripe from the eye to the back of the head; long neck; grey body; long legs. During the breeding season grey herons grow long, thin feathers on the neck and breast and two long black feathers on the back of the head. The beak changes colour from dull yellow-orange to a bright pink.
Immature: greyer plumage, duller beak. **In flight:** slow wing beats on bowed wings, neck tucked up and legs trailing beyond short tail. Wings and back grey with darker primaries and secondaries.

Voice guide: When it takes off or is disturbed it gives a loud *frraank* call. Some of the sounds of adults and young at the nest, heard at any time of day or night, are like a fairy-tale monster or someone getting sick!

Diet: mainly fish, frogs, small animals and occasionally insects.
Food to put out: none usually but it may take cat or dog food on the ground during severe winter weather.
Nesting season: mid-February to early May.
Nest location: on the top of tall trees, occasionally on low bushes and on the ground on small islands. Usually nests in colonies called heronries, which it frequents from January until late summer.
Nest: a platform of twigs and branches, occasionally lined with fine strands of plant material. Each year the nest is repaired and more twigs and branches are added, so older nests can become very big. Male brings the material and female makes the nest.
Eggs: three to four, 61mm, large matt pale green-blue eggs.
Incubation period: 27 days by female and male.
Fledging time: About 52 days, fed by both parents.
Number of broods reared per year: one.
Nest box: no.
Average Lifespan: five years.
Oldest known individual: 23 years.

Confusion species
None

Im.

Ad.

Im.

Ad.

ℹ General information

Often referred to as a 'crane' or 'Johnny-the-Bog', the grey heron is Ireland's tallest bird. It can often be seen standing motionless, stalking its prey on lake edges, in rivers and streams or on the coast. Usually attracted to gardens by unprotected ornamental ponds containing goldfish, which it can eat in large numbers if available. When in flight it is sometimes chased by crows and gulls. Bird-Watch Ireland's Countryside Bird Survey indicates a slight decline in recent years.

Sparrowhawk *Accipiter nisus*

Spioróg

Length = 28–38cm
Wingspan = 60–75cm
All-Ireland population: 17,500 individuals

Rank
29
Garden
Bird Survey

Seen in
17%
of gardens
in Ireland

Identification features

About the size of a rook. **Male:** blue-grey above; barred white and orange below; underside of tail, broadly barred light and dark grey-brown; short, pale hooked beak with a dark tip; bright yellow eye and yellow legs. **Female:** larger than the male; dark grey-brown above; pale supercilium; barred white and brown below. **In flight:** broad blunt-ended wings; long slightly round-ended tail; rapid wing beats with short glides; soars but does not hover.

Voice guide: Varied repertoire during the breeding season including a loud high *wa-kaa-kaa-kaa*, each phrase lasting about two seconds, followed by a brief pause and repeat. When the young are begging for food they make a high squeaking *weee-weee-weee*. Silent outside the breeding season.

Diet: mainly small birds, which it catches by surprise. Females, because of their larger size, can catch much larger birds than the male.

Food to put out: none.

Nesting Season: early April to late May.

Nest Location: Nests in trees, usually in woodlands.

Nest: an almost flat platform of twigs, roughly lined with green leaves and small twigs. Built mainly by the female.

Eggs: four to five, 40mm, matt white eggs, sometimes tinted blue with rusty red-brown and occasionally purple-blue blotches and spots varying in pattern, laid at intervals of a few days.

Incubation period: 34–40 days by the female.

Fledging time: 30 days, fed by both parents. Depends on the parents for food for about a month or so after fledging.

Number of broods reared per year: one.

Nest box: no.

Average lifespan: three years.

Oldest known individual: 17 years.

M.

Juv.

M.

F.

F.

General information

The sparrowhawk and kestrel are the most abundant birds of prey in Ireland. The sparrowhawk employs two main hunting techniques: circling high over woodlands, like a tiny vulture, looking for small birds below; and hunting along hedgerows and in gardens where it ambushes its prey. Almost all birds seen in gardens have been hunted by this species. There is some evidence in recent years to suggest that the sparrowhawk is declining as a breeding species in Ireland, though the cause is unknown.

Confusion species

Kestrel (p. 84) has more pointed wings and when viewed from above is warm red-brown in colour. Prefers open country, rarely seen in gardens.

Kestrel *Falco tinnunculus*

Windhover   Pocaire gaoithe | J | F | M | A | M | J | J | A | S | O | N | D |

Length = 33–39cm
Wingspan = 65–80cm
All-Ireland population: 20,000
individuals

Rank
37
Garden
Bird Survey

Seen in
7%
of gardens
in Ireland

Identification features

Slightly bigger than a jackdaw. **Male:** grey head; grey tail with a black band on the end; dark primaries; rust-red wing coverts and back; body buff with dark streaking; underwing pale; short dark hooked beak with a yellow base. Legs long and yellow. **Female and immature:** duller brown instead of rusty red above; more heavily streaked below. **In flight:** Flies with deep wing beats and glides. When hunting circles with tail spread and then hovers over one place before dropping from the air onto its prey.

Voice guide: vocal during the breeding season, near its nest; a loud sharp rapid *kee-kee-kee-keee*.

Diet: mainly small mammals such as mice and shrews, occasionally taking small birds and insects.

Food to put out: none.

Nesting season: mid-April to mid-May.

Nest location: Nests in a wide variety of habitats with flat ledges, e.g. old trees, ruins, cliff ledges and even on large buildings.

Nest: Does not usually build a nest; will use any flat ledge and sometimes old nests of other species.

Eggs: four to five, 40mm, matt white, cream or buff eggs with many spots, flecks and blotches of varying shades of brown; eggs laid at intervals of a few days.

Incubation period: 28 days, mainly by the female.

Fledging time: 35 days; male brings most of the food and the female feeds the nestlings. Young dependent on the parents for food for a further month or so.

Number of broods reared per year: one.

Nest box: large open-fronted box.

Average lifespan: no data available.

Oldest known individual: 15 years.

Ad. F.

Ad. M.

 Ad. F.

Juv.

General information

The kestrel is a perfect example of how a bird can be identified by its jizz alone (see glossary). Its ability to hover in the air in most wind conditions, with tail spread and wings held high, makes it unique among Irish birds of prey. Breeds throughout the country and can often be seen hunting next to roads and motorways, especially where there are large grass margins. BirdWatch Ireland's Countryside Bird Survey indicates a slight decline in population in recent years.

Confusion species

Sparrowhawk (p. 82) in flight has rounded wing tips and rarely hovers. Dark brown or blue-grey upperparts

Black-headed Gull *Larus ridibundus*

Faoileán an chaipín/Sléibhín

J F M A M J J A S O N D

Length = 35–38cm
Wingspan = 94–105cm
All-Ireland population: 53,000 breeding pairs

Rank
41
Garden Bird Survey

Seen in
5%
of gardens in Ireland

Identification features

A small gull, about the size of a rook. **Summer:** wings and back pale grey; white leading edge and black tips to the primaries; head chocolate-brown, not black; rest of body white; legs and beak deep red. **Winter:** same as summer, but head is white with a dark spot behind the eye. **Immature:** brown on the wings; dark band on the end of the tail; legs orange-yellow; beak pale brown-yellow, black tip; identical in size and shape to the adults. **In flight:** pale grey on back and wings; white leading edge to outer primaries forming a long thin white triangle (above and below) with a black trailing edge. Immature birds have a dark trailing edge to the secondaries, brown on the wing coverts and a dark tail band. Wings very pointed. Will sometimes circle and soar in small flocks, in vulture-like fashion over ploughed fields and in pursuit of flying ants.

Voice guide: Can be very noisy, especially when feeding. Calls are higher in pitch than the larger gulls, and include a thin-sounding drawn-out *kaaww,* and also a softer chatter.

Diet: a wide variety of prey items including insects, earthworms, also plant material and food scraps from restaurants and takeaways.

Food to put out: bread and kitchen scraps.

Nesting season: mid-April to mid-May.

Nest location: Nests on the ground in colonies, mainly on islands on inland lakes and bogs but occasionally along the coast.

Nest: a shallow scrape on the ground surrounded by plant material.

Eggs: two to three, 52mm, slightly glossy eggs, colour varies from pale brown to olive green and is covered with flecks spots and blotches of dark brown, olive or black which may vary in pattern.

Incubation period: 25 days, by female and male.

Fledging time: 35 days, fed by both parents. Soon after hatching young are able to run around but stay at or near the nest.

Number of broods reared per year: one.

Nest box: no.

Average lifespan: six years.

Oldest known individual: 29 years.

Ad. Br.

1st W.

Ad. NBr.

d. NBr.

1st W.

General information

The black-headed gull is the gull most likely to visit gardens. It might be surprising to learn that, unlike most other seagulls, black-headed gulls breed mainly in the midlands, west and north of the country on bogs, marshes, brackish lagoons and islands. From July onwards, adults and young birds, with their noticeable brown marking on the nape and side of the breast, begin to appear away from the breeding colonies, especially in estuaries. It is more common on the east and south coasts. Large numbers come here each winter from Britain, Scandinavia and Eastern Europe. Will avail of an easy meal from fast-food outlet refuse, even feeding at night along city streets. More typically found on a mudflat, playing field or refuse tip, behind fishing boats or a tractor ploughing a field.

Confusion species

Herring Gull (p. 88). May resemble other gull species at a distance but a clear view of the beak and leg colour of an adult will separate it from other gull species.

Herring Gull *Larus argentatus*

Faoileán scadán

Length = 55–67cm
Wingspan = 130–148cm
All-Ireland population: 45,000
breeding pairs

Rank
45
Garden
Bird Survey

Seen in
3%
of gardens
in Ireland

Identification features

Much larger than the black-headed gull. **Adult:** body white, back and wings light grey, black and white wing tips; legs pink; beak yellow with a red spot; eyes yellow. In winter, head and neck can become mottled grey-brown. **Immature:** dirty grey-brown markings on head and body; wings a complex pattern of browns, black and buff, primaries and secondaries mainly dark brown; beak and tail band black; gradual plumage change over four years to reach adult plumage. **In flight:** In strong winds will glide on bowed wings high over land and sea. Light blue-grey back and wings above with black and white wing tips (much more black than white). Thin white trailing edge to the wing. Immatures have varying amounts of brown on the body and wings, usually with no white at the wing tips.

Voice guide: Calls include a loud repeated *kuwaa* and a laugh-like *agah-ga-ga*.

Diet: a broad diet, eating mainly meat in the form of fish or carrion. Will occasionally come into gardens where kitchen scraps are put out for birds.

Food to put out: bread and kitchen scraps.

Nesting season: late April and May.

Nest location: Usually nests in colonies on or near the top of sea cliffs and offshore islands on rocky ledges, in long grass or under tall weeds. Will sometimes nest on rooftops in urban areas near the sea.

Nest: a hollow surrounded by seaweed and other plant material.

Eggs: two to three, 70mm, large matt pale brown or green-brown eggs with variable large spots and blotches of dark brown or black, eggs laid at intervals of a few days.

Incubation period: 28 days, by both parents.

Fledging time: 38 days, fed by both parents. Young can run around soon after hatching but usually stay near the nest.

Number of broods reared per year: one.

Nest box: no.

Average lifespan: 19 years.

Oldest known individual: 31 years.

Yr.

Ad. Br.

1st W.

Ad. Br.

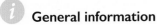

General information

This large gull is found not only all along our coast but also inland, especially in winter. It is a scavenger, so will be found anywhere there is a possibility of a free meal, such as at rubbish dumps, around fishing boats or along the shoreline. The herring gull is very noisy and defends its territory during the breeding season with great energy. It will dive-bomb anything that intrudes, attacking with beak or wings. The Irish population has dropped dramatically in the last 30 years.

Confusion species

Black-headed gull (p. 86) is much smaller, with a dark spot behind the eye, dark brown hood in summer, and thin red beak and legs on adults.

Feral Pigeon *Columba livia*

Colm aille

J F M A M J J A S O N D

Length = 31–33cm
Wingspan = 65–67cm
All-Ireland population: 50,000 breeding pairs

Rank
28
Garden
Bird Survey

Seen in
26%
of gardens
in Ireland

Identification features

Smaller than the woodpigeon and stockier than the collared dove. The feral pigeon does not have a consistent plumage pattern, with individuals varying from almost black to pure white. The plumage pattern is often asymmetric with patches of white, brown or dark grey. Feral pigeons are a familiar sight in city squares and around grain stores and farmyards. Racing pigeons and feral pigeons are one and the same. **In flight:** Because they are usually seen in flocks, the most noticeable feature is the lack of a distinct pattern common to all individuals. Some show a classic grey plumage with twin black wing bars and white rump, reminiscent of the wild rock dove.

Voice guide: a variety of soft cooing sounds.

Diet: usually seeds, bread and kitchen scraps.
Food to put out: seed and bread on the ground.
Nesting season: March to September, almost all year round in urban areas.
Nest location: Usually nests in loose colonies in suburban and urban areas. The nest is usually built on a ledge, often in derelict buildings or large warehouses.
Nest: may range from a few loose twigs to a more substantial nest of twigs and other plant material.
Eggs: two, 39mm long, slightly shiny white eggs.
Incubation Period: 17–19 days, by both parents.
Fledging time: 30–33 days, fed by both parents and continues to be fed by the parents for a short while after fledging.
Number of broods reared per year: three to five or more.
Nest box: large hole-entrance box.
Average lifespan: three years.
Oldest known individual: seven years.

ℹ️ General information

The feral pigeon is the descendant of the rock dove. A bird of sea cliffs now only found in remote areas of the west coast. It was originally domesticated for its meat. Monasteries, castles and large estates built special structures called dovecotes for housing rock doves. Because of their strong homing instincts they were also used for sending messages and were sometimes called carrier pigeons. Today, feral pigeons are mainly used for racing; tired or lost individuals will sometimes turn up in the garden especially during the summer, and are especially tame.

Confusion species

Young woodpigeons (p. 92) can look similar but have white crescents on the upper wings, visible in flight. Stock Dove (not illustrated/no species profile) is similar in appearance but is typically associated with arable farms and not usually a visitor to gardens.

Woodpigeon *Columba palumbus*

Colm coille

Length = 40–42cm
Wingspan = 75–80cm
All-Ireland population: 2.6 million
individuals

Rank
15
Garden
Bird Survey

Seen in
71%
of gardens
in Ireland

Identification features

Slightly smaller and heavier than a rook. **Adult:** pure white neck
patches and wing crescents on the wings; pink-grey breast, rest of
body greyer; rump and lower back pale blue-grey; tail grey with a
dark band on the end, more clearly marked grey and black below;
very fat-looking; small head; short red legs; pale yellow and pink
beak; pale cream iris. **Immature:** like an adult, but lacks the white
neck patches. **In flight:** when flying out of trees it can make a loud
racket as its wings hit leaves and branches. Its display flight, used to
defend its territory, involves a steep flight upwards ending in loud
wing claps and a downward glide, sometimes repeated.

Voice guide: Its call is a series of loud cooing notes sounding like,
'Take two, John, take two'. This phrase is often repeated several times
and may start in the middle of a phrase.

Diet: seeds, leaves, berries, buds, beechmast (beechnuts), acorns and
root crops.
Food to put out: seed and bread on the ground.
Nesting season: early March to late August.
Nest location: Usually nests in trees or large shrubs.
Nest: usually flat, not very thick and made of twigs. Mainly built by
the female.
Eggs: two to three, 41mm long, slightly shiny white eggs.
Incubation period: 16 days, by both parents.
Fledging Time: 30–34 days, fed by both parents.
Number of broods reared per year: one to three.
Nest box: no.
Average lifespan: three years.
Oldest known individual: 17 years.

Ad.

Ad.

Juv.

General information

As the name suggests, the woodpigeon usually nests in trees and bushes but will also nest in any vegetated area, even on the ground in some locations. Small numbers come here from Britain and mainland Europe in the winter. Known to cause damage to crops, especially during the winter, when it will feed on kale, turnips and clover. It also visits vegetable patches early in the morning and can clean out a whole bed of newly emerging plants very quickly without being seen. In autumn, flocks of up to 15,000 have been recorded and with so much food available, survival rates for young are very high. It has been conservatively estimated that as many as 3 million woodpigeons are in Ireland each autumn. Rather than feed their young insects, pigeons feed them a milk formed from sloughing off fluid-filled cells in the crop lining. It is more nutritious than human or cow's milk. BirdWatch Ireland's Countryside Bird Survey indicates a slight increase in population in recent years.

Confusion species

Feral pigeon (p. 90) comes in all patterns and colours from almost all black to pure white or rusty red. Does not have the white neck patches or wing crescents. Found mainly in urban areas. Stock dove (not illustrated/no species profile) rarely found in gardens. Lacks the white neck patches and wing crescents and is typically associated with arable farms.

Collared Dove *Streptopelia decaocto*

Fearán baicdhubh

J F M A M J J A S O N D

Length = 31–33cm
Wingspan = 47–55cm
All-Ireland population: 260,000 individuals

Rank

17

Garden Bird Survey

Seen in

67%

of gardens in Ireland

Identification features

Slim, sand-coloured dove. **Upperparts:** brown back and inner wing, dark brown-black outer primaries. **Underside:** pale grey-brown underside, distinctive but not always noticeable black half-collar at base of the neck; beak short, thin and dark; eyes dark red; legs short and powdery pink. **In flight:** files straight with fast jerky wing beats. In display flight it glides with stiff, slightly down-curved wings and fanned tail, clearly showing the pale underwing and white undertail with a black band at the base.

Voice guide: Its call is a gentle '*cooing*' sound phrased like '*can yoouuu coo*' repeated two or more times.

Diet: mainly seeds of weeds and cereal crops. Will sometimes eat shoots and insects.
Food to put out: seed and bread.
Nesting season: March to September.
Nest location: Nests in trees and sometimes ledges on buildings.
Nest: a light flat platform made of twigs. Mainly built by the female.
Eggs: two to three, 31mm long, shiny white eggs.
Incubation period: 16 days by both parents.
Fledging time: 17–19 days, fed by both parents.
Number of broods reared per year: three to six.
Nest box: no.
Average lifespan: three years.
Oldest known individual: 16 years.

Confusion species
None.

Juv.

Ad.

ⓘ General information

The collared dove is a recent colonist of Ireland. In 1930 the nearest breeding birds were in Yugoslavia. Following an amazing population explosion, 29 years later it was breeding over most of Europe and reached Ireland in 1959 when it was first recorded in Counties Down, Dublin and Galway. It first bred in Counties Kildare, Kilkenny and Louth as recently as 1969. Now it is estimated that as many as 30,000 pairs breed in Ireland. Less likely to be found over high ground and more open countryside. A regular but wary visitor to bird tables. Often perches on overhead wires and lamp posts where it delivers its monotonous song. BirdWatch Ireland's Countryside Bird Survey indicates a slight increase in population in recent years.

Barn Owl *Tyto alba*

Scréachóg reilige

Length = 37–39cm
Wingspan = 85–93cm
All-Ireland population: 400 breeding pairs

Rank
50+
Garden Bird Survey

Seen in
<1%
of gardens in Ireland

Identification features

About the size of a jackdaw. Flat, white, heart-shaped face with large black eyes. **Upperparts** deep yellow-buff with small dark flecks. **Underside** white; legs long with large taloned feet; looks 'knock-kneed' when perched; no ear tufts. **In flight:** silent; blunt head; short tail; wings broad and round-tipped; wing beats jerky and stiff.

Voice guide: The quietest of our owls but occasionally makes a loud shriek. The young make a hissing noise. The hooting call some-times attributed to the barn owl and heard on television and radio is actually made by the tawny owl, a species common in Britain but which does not occur in Ireland.

Diet: It usually eats wood mice and pygmy shrews. In suburban and urban areas its diet includes small birds, house mice and rats. Bank voles, where they occur, form 20 per cent to 25 per cent of prey items.

Food to put out: none.

Nesting season: April to June.

Nest location: holes in large trees, ledges in farm buildings, on ruins and occasionally in quarries.

Nest: Does not make a nest but will make a depression in any twigs and debris, if present.

Eggs: four to seven, 39–40mm, smooth, matt white, very round eggs.

Incubation period: 30–35 days, by the female while being fed by the male.

Fledging time: 54–62 days, fed by both parents. After fledging will be fed by the parents for a further two weeks or so.

Number of broods reared per year: one to two.

Nest box: tea-chest type box for barns and covered areas; 'A' frame box for trees and outdoor use.

Average lifespan: three to four years.

Oldest known individual: 17 years.

Ad.

Ad.

Ad.

Ad.

chick

ⓘ General information

Ireland's best-known yet most-threatened owl, it is usually seen briefly in the beam of car headlights or a street lamp. A largely nocturnal bird, it rarely hunts by day and is the source of many a 'ghost sighting'. The best chance of seeing one is either in the headlights of a car at night or at dawn or dusk hunting along a field or woodland edge or riverbank during the breeding season. Sometimes killed by cars and found dead by the roadside. It is a Red-listed *Bird of Conservation Concern In Ireland* due to a decline of over 50 per cent in their population during the past 25 years caused by a combination of factors, including lack of suitable nest sites, intensification of farming, and the use of rodenticides. It is more numerous in the southern half of the country.

Confusion species

Long-eared owl (p. 98) is a slimmer and much darker bird with orange irises and diagnostic ear tufted on the head.

Long-eared Owl *Asio otus*

Ceann cait

J F M A M J J A S O N D

Length = 35–37cm
Wingspan = 84–95cm
All-Ireland population: 1,100–3,600
breeding pairs

Seen in

<1%

of gardens
in Ireland

Identification features

A little larger than a jackdaw. **Upperparts:** a complex pattern of light and dark browns, grey, and some white spots on the inner wing area. Eyes fiery red-orange; feather tufts that look like ears. **Underside:** light brown with heavy dark streaking. **In flight:** Blunt head, short tail, broad round-ended wings. Very stiff, jerky flight, indistinct dark patch on the leading edge of the outer wing. Mainly nocturnal.

Voice guide: Like most owls, usually silent but during the breeding season the male makes a low moaning *whoo-oooo-oooo* call; also makes squeaks and clapping sounds. Young have a begging call, often heard during the day: a monotonous call reminiscent of a squeaking gate.

Diet: Feeds at night, mainly on wood mice and rats and occasionally small birds.
Food to put out: none.
Nesting season: mid-March to early May.
Nest location: usually in woods and conifer plantations.
Nest: Does not usually build a nest itself, preferring to use an old large abandoned nest.
Eggs: four to five, 41mm long, slightly shiny white eggs.
Incubation period: 28 days, usually by the female.
Fledging time: 30–32 days.
Number of broods reared per year: one.
Nest box: platform.
Average lifespan: four years.
Oldest known individual: 12 years.

Confusion species

Barn owl (p. 96) has much paler plumage; white, heart-shaped 'face' and dark eyes.

Ad.

Juv.

Ad.

ℹ️ **General information**

Our most common owl and yet probably not seen as often as the barn owl. It occurs wherever there are small stands of trees with open countryside nearby. It has also become associated with forestry plantations and appears to be increasing in numbers. Small numbers migrate here from the continent each winter.

Swift *Apus apus*

Gabhlán gaoithe

Length = 16–17cm
Wingspan = 42–48cm
All-Ireland population: 116,000 individuals

Recorded in
13%
of squares in the
Countryside Bird Survey

Identification features

Smaller than a starling. Never seen on the ground or perching in the open. All black plumage, except for a pale throat, visible only at close range. **In flight:** dashing flight on long, scythe-shaped wings; stiff wing beats thought by some to alternate; very short forked tail which can look pointed. Swifts often gather at dusk in large screeching flocks, high in the sky, when they are sometimes heard but not seen.

Voice guide: A distinctive sound of summer is a group of swifts, screaming with high-pitched buzzing calls, speeding over church spires and low around houses and streets.

Diet: mainly flying insects.
Food to put out: none.
Nesting season: May to July.
Nest location: Nests in the eaves of buildings, usually two or more storeys tall, and also on cliff ledges where available.
Nest: a shallow cup made of plant material caught in flight and glued together by saliva.
Eggs: two to three, 25mm, matt white or pale cream eggs.
Incubation period: 23 days, by both parents.
Fledging time: Young are fed by both parents. Because the swift's food supply is so unpredictable the young are able to go without food for some time and so may fledge in anything from 38 to 56 days.
Number of broods reared per year: one.
Nest box: special hole-entrance box.
Average lifespan: nine years.
Oldest known individual: 18 years.

Confusion species

Starlings (p. 164) in flight have relatively short broad-based wings, a noticeable beak and do not glide so much.

ⓘ General information

Lands only at its nest, to rear young and even sleeps on the wing by letting half of its brain sleep at a time. It also mates on the wing. Because of its adaptation to an aerial existence, if a swift becomes grounded it is usually unable to take off again. It is one of the latest of our summer visitors to arrive and the earliest to depart, coming at the beginning of May and leaving in August. It feeds on insects, which it catches by flying quickly with its mouth wide open. Insects are stored in a ball in the crop or throat pouch for feeding young. Can roam far to find food. Scarcer in the west of Ireland. BirdWatch Ireland's Countryside Bird Survey indicates a decrease in population in recent years.

Great Spotted Woodpecker
Dendrocopos major

Mórchnagaire breac

J F M A M J J A S O N D

Length = 23–26cm
Wingspan = 38–44cm
All-Ireland population: a few hundred breeding pairs in 2016

Rank
50+
Garden Bird Survey

Seen in
<1%
of gardens in Ireland

Identification features

About the size of a Mistle Thrush or Blackbird. Shy and often remains in canopy. Usually located by distinctive (once learnt) call. Forages on trunks of trees in an upright position, leaning back on short tail. Black and white plumage, with distinctive deep signal-red vent, otherwise white below. Two obvious white shoulder patches on dark back. Male has small red blob on nape. Juveniles have a distinctive red crown.

In flight: Deep undulations in otherwise direct, strong flight; black wings and tail sides have white barring.

Voice guide: A distinctive, short, sharp, 'kick', sometimes repeated. Drums in spring, a resonant, far-carrying, short, knocking roll with sudden ending. Young beg noisily from the nest hole before fledging: '*vivivivivi*.'

Diet: insects, tree seeds and occasionally birds' eggs or nestlings.

Food to put out: peanuts, suet balls.

Nesting season: March to late June.

Nest location: Nests in an excavated hole in a tree, usually three or more metres up: in Ireland has colonised oak forest in the east of the country, but also occurs in pine, ash and birch.

Nest: no nest material apart from wood chippings in self-excavated nest hole.

Eggs: four to seven, broadly elliptical, glossy white eggs.

Incubation period: 16 days.

Fledging time: Young are fed by both parents, fledged in about 20 days.

Number of broods reared per year: one.

Nest box: known to use a starling type nest box elsewhere in its wide range.

Average lifespan: five years.

Oldest known individual: 10 years.

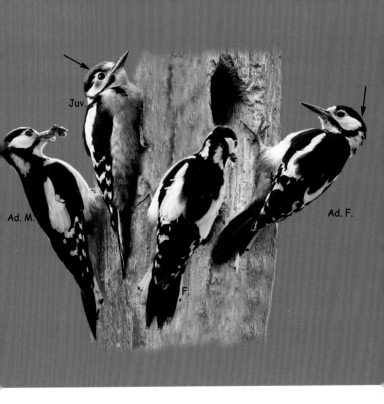

Juv.

Ad. M.

F.

Ad. F.

General information

A very widespread species across Europe. It is thought that the recent colonisation of Ireland (first proof of breeding in 2006) is fuelled by a population expansion in Britain, where a 400 per cent population increase was recorded between 1967 and 2010. Before 2006 it was known only in Ireland as a rare winter vagrant, mainly from northern Europe where individuals are migratory. First recorded breeding in Counties Down and Wicklow with range expansion evident and expected, south and westwards. Winter feeding in gardens may well sustain birds in hard weather.

Confusion species

None. Once seen well, relatively straightforward to identify.

Swallow *Hirundo rustica*

Fáinleog

J F M A M J J A S O N D

Length = 19–22cm
Wingspan = 32–34cm
All-Ireland population: 5.8 million individuals

Recorded in
89%
of squares in the
Countryside Bird Survey

Identification features

Upperparts: blue-black with a metallic sheen on the back and head; long outer tail feathers, longer in the males than the females or young; white spots forming a crescent near the end of the tail, most noticeable from below. **Underparts:** slightly hooked, very short, broad, black beak; forehead and throat red-brown, paler on young birds; black breast band; white or cream belly and undertail; tiny, very short black legs. **In flight:** agile; dips, dives and glides over watercourses and open country. Deeply forked tail, longer in male birds.

Voice guide: The call is a short *whit* sound. The song is a series of fast twittering sounds interspersed with chattering and whistling notes.

Diet: flying insects, especially large flies such as bluebottles, hoverflies and horseflies caught in flight.

Food to put out: none.

Nesting season: May to August.

Nest location: on rafters and walls in barns and outhouses; has also been recorded nesting in caves.

Nest: half-cup nest of mud and straw mixed with saliva. Built by both male and female.

Eggs: four to five, 20mm, glossy white eggs, lightly spotted all over with flecks ranging in colour from rusty brown to dark grey.

Incubation Period: 17 days, usually by the female.

Fledging time: 21 days; fed by both parents, sometimes in mid-air after learning to fly.

Number of broods reared per year: one or two, rarely three.

Nest box: platform or artificial half-cup.

Average lifespan: three years.

Oldest known individual: 11 years.

Ad.

Juv.

Juv.

Ad.

chicks
in
nest

ⓘ General information

Studies have shown that females will choose to mate with males with the most symmetrical tails as these are thought to be the healthiest individuals. A bird of the farmed countryside, rarely seen in the centre of cities or towns. In August and September swallows gather in large flocks before beginning a southerly migration along our coasts, gathering over reed beds where they roost. As many as 30,000 birds have been counted at these pre-migration roosts on occasions. It winters in southern Africa. There has been a slight decline in numbers in recent years and pesticides and modern farm design (no more gaps at the top of barn doors) may be the cause. Up to the 19th century, was thought to hibernate underwater in rivers and lakes in the winter.

Confusion species

House martin (p. 106) has a square white rump patch, all white underside and very short, slightly forked tail. Prefers nesting on the outside of buildings.

House Martin *Delichon urbica*

Gabhlán binne

J F M A M J J A S O N D

Length = 12–13cm
Wingspan = 26–28cm
All-Ireland population: 730,000 individuals

Recorded in
30%
of squares in the
Countryside Bird Survey

Identification features

Smaller than a swallow. **Upperparts:** black with metallic blue sheen; obvious square white rump patch; short black forked tail; very short black beak. **Underside:** body white, wings and tail black; very short white feet. **In flight:** white rump patch; agile, flutters and glides; black and white appearance.

Voice guide: call a loud clear *prreet*.

Diet: flying insects, especially flies and aphids.

Food to put out: none.

Nesting season: May and June.

Nest location: under an overhanging ledge. Its preference for nesting under the eaves of houses explains its name though it will also use natural sites such as cliffs. Like the swift it can be found nesting in the centre of towns and villages.

Nest: mud collected from pool edges and plant material, shaped into small balls and cemented together with saliva to form a half-cup. The same nest can be used for several years, with ongoing repairs. Built by both male and female.

Eggs: four to five, 19 mm, slightly shiny, usually unmarked white eggs. Incubation period: 17 days, by both parents.

Fledging time: 22 days, young fed by both parents. Fledged young from the first brood may help feed the young of the second brood.

Number of broods reared per year: two.

Nest box: hole entrance or artificial half-cup.

Average lifespan: two years.

Oldest known individual: seven years.

Confusion species

Swallow (p. 104) has longer forked tail; all dark above, except for small white spots on the tail; red-brown throat; black breast band. Prefers to nest inside sheltered outbuildings.

nest

Ad.

ℹ️ General information

A summer visitor that feeds on the wing, though will land on the ground at puddles to collect mud for nest building. It is more common in the eastern half of the island. It arrives in late April and early May and departs for Africa in September and October. It often nests colonially, with a number of nests under the same eave, usually near the apex of the roof. BirdWatch Ireland's Countryside Bird Survey indicates a slight increase in population in recent years.

Meadow Pipit *Anthus pratensis*

Riabhóg mhóna

Length = 14–15cm
Wingspan = 23–24cm
All-Ireland population: 1.7 million individuals

Rank
48
Garden Bird Survey

Seen in
3%
of gardens in Ireland

Identification features

Same size as a robin, but slimmer in shape. Superficially resembles a miniature thrush. **Upperparts:** head dull brown; back streaked black and brown; tail long with thin white outer tail feathers. **Underside:** pale buff throat, black streaking on cream breast, flanks and upper belly; short fine beak and long pink legs. **In flight:** weak; bouncing flight, white outer tail feathers usually visible as it takes off. **Voice guide:** Its call is a high sharp *weeep*, loudest when disturbed or alarmed. Its song is complex, starting with speeding up, high *seep* notes and ending with a melodious trill. Usually sung while rising from the ground and ends with the bird dropping to the ground with fluttering wings and tail raised high, referred to as parachuting.

Diet: mostly insects, some seeds in winter; almost always feeds on the ground.

Food to put out: none.

Nesting season: mid-April to mid-June.

Nest location: Nests on the ground in habitat ranging from coast to mountain areas, preferring rough pasture and long grass.

Nest: cup-shaped, made of dry grass and other plant material, well hidden in long grass.

Eggs: three to four, 20mm, shiny cream or pale grey eggs covered with dense fine flecks ranging in colour from grey-green to dark brown.

Incubation period: 14 days, usually by the female.

Fledging time: 13 days, fed by both parents.

Number of broods reared per year: two.

Nest box: no.

Average lifespan: three years.

Oldest known individual: seven years.

Juv.

in parachute
song flight

Ad.
(autumn)

Ad.
(spring)

General information

Like the skylark, the meadow pipit is a ground-loving bird of open countryside and is one of our most abundant and wide-spread species. Usually seen singly or in small loose flocks, though large flocks in autumn are not rare. Very common on the western seaboard, less so in the east. Regularly parasitised by the cuckoo, which will lay its egg in the nests of unsuspecting host meadow pipits. In winter, numbers increase in the south and on low ground, and are more noticeable on the coast. Only occasionally visits gardens, especially on high ground. Some Irish meadow pipits migrate to southern Europe in winter and birds from continental Europe join those that remain in Ireland. BirdWatch Ireland's Countryside Bird Survey indicates a decrease in population in recent years.

Confusion species

Song thrush (p. 128) is much larger, and does not have white outer tail feathers.

Grey Wagtail *Motacilla cinerea*

Glasóg liath

Length = 18–19cm
Wingspan = 25–26cm
All-Ireland population: 84,000 individuals

Rank
33
Garden
Bird Survey

Seen in
11%
of gardens
in Ireland

Identification features

Slightly bigger than a robin. **Male:** grey head, mantle and back; thin white supercilium; yellow rump; tail as long as its body, black with white outer feathers; black chin and throat in summer; breast, belly and undertail coverts yellow. **Female:** resembles male but has a white throat and belly; yellow breast and undertail. **In flight:** undulating flight pattern; noticeable white wing bar and white outer tail feathers.

Voice guide: The call is a short loud descending *tee-tee*, made when disturbed or in flight.

Diet: It feeds on insects, mainly flies, which it catches by flying out from a perch to grab the insect with a flurry of wings and a spread tail clearly showing the white outer tail feathers.

Food to put out: none.

Nesting season: end March to mid-June.

Nest location: usually built on a ledge near fresh water.

Nest: cup-shaped nest made of plant material, lined with hair and feathers.

Eggs: four to five, 19mm, shiny pale blue or light grey eggs with very fine flecks of dark grey or grey brown, sometimes dark streaks.

Incubation period: 12–14 days, usually by the female.

Fledging time: 14 days, fed by both parents.

Number of broods reared per year: one to two.

Nest box: open-front box.

Average lifespan: no data available.

Oldest known individual: seven years.

Confusion species

Pied wagtail (p. 112) has similar shape, a white face and no yellow in its plumage.

Br. F.

Juv.

Br. M.

Br. F.

ⓘ General information

The grey wagtail is found all over Ireland and is never seen far from water, often close to farmyards. During the breeding season it prefers fast-flowing rivers and streams, especially when bordered with broadleaved trees. In the winter it is more numerous in the south-east of the island and can be seen on the coast and anywhere near watercourses. BirdWatch Ireland's Countryside Bird Survey indicates a significant decrease in population in recent years.

Pied Wagtail *Motacilla alba*

Willy Wagtail
Siubháinín an bhóthair

Length = 18cm
Wingspan = 27–28cm
All-Ireland population: 500,000 individuals

Rank
22
Garden
Bird Survey

Seen in
49%
of gardens
in Ireland

Identification features

Slightly larger than a robin. **Male:** upperparts black, except for two white wing bars; white face; black forehead and throat; black bib on the breast; belly and undertail coverts white; flanks dark grey; long black tail with white outer tail feathers, wagged frequently. **Female and immature:** grey mantle, back and upper wing coverts. **In flight:** undulating, short bursts of wing beats followed by dipping glides with wings closed.

Voice guide Call is an explosive high *tchi-zzik* or *tsli-vitt.* Song, which includes call notes, is longer and twittering.

Diet: mainly small insects.
Food to put out: Occasionally eats bread on the ground.
Nesting season: mid-April to the end of July.
Nest location: Prefers to nest in holes or covered ledges ranging from trees and walls to drain pipes and sometimes old nests of other species.
Nest: a cup-shaped nest, usually built by the female, made of plant material lined with feathers, hair or wool.
Eggs: four to five, 21mm, shiny pale blue or light grey eggs with very fine flecks of dark grey or grey-brown.
Incubation period: 13 days, mainly by the female.
Fledging time: four days, fed by both parents.
Number of broods reared per year: one to two.
Nest box: open-front box.
Average lifespan: two years.
Oldest known individual: 11 years.

NBr. M.

NBr. F.

Br. M.

Juv.

General information

A very common bird in Ireland, often referred to as 'willy wagtail'. This bird is as much at home in the centre of cities as on open bogland. Sometimes seen removing dead insects from wing mirrors and radiator grilles of cars, and has even been known to nest in cars. In the winter, roosts in large flocks in trees and ruins, or on flat rooftops. In large towns and cities these roosts often contain hundreds of birds.

Confusion species

Adult grey wagtail (p. 110) has lemon yellow on the undersides; young lack black on the breast.

Waxwing *Bombycilla garrulus*

Síodeiteach

J F M A M J J A S O N D

Length = 18cm
Wingspan = 33–35cm
Winter population: no data

Rank
43
Garden
Bird Survey

Seen in
4%
of gardens
in Ireland

Identification features

Slightly smaller than a starling. Very exotic looking, unlikely to be confused with any other Irish garden bird. Overall it looks pale pink-brown. **Adult:** short beak, orange-brown face with black around the eye and on the chin, prominent crest, small red spots on the wings. Bright yellow on the tips of the primaries and on the end of the tail. Bright orange-brown undertail. **Immature:** very similar to the adult but lacks white on the primaries and red spots on the wings. **In flight:** Similar to starling, usually slightly undulating with rapid wing beats.

Voice guide Flocks can be very noisy. The call is an unusual and distinctive high-pitched trill reminiscent of tinkling bells or a sound recording played at high speed.

Diet: In the summer mainly small insects, especially mosquitoes. In the winter it feeds on fruit and berries, especially rowan berries and whatever berry sources remain at the end of an Irish winter.

Food to put out: Occasionally takes fruit and kitchen scraps.

Nesting season: mid-May to end June.

Nest location: conifer and birch forests of northern Scandinavia, Siberia and North America. The nest is usually on the branch of a conifer tree. The nest is cup-shaped, made of twigs and moss and lined with down. Built by both the male and female.

Eggs: four to six, 25mm long, shiny pale blue or light grey eggs with sparse fine dark spots and flecks.

Incubation period: 12–14 days, by the female.

Fledging time: 16 days, fed by both parents.

Number of broods reared per year: one.

Nest box: none.

Average lifespan: no information.

Oldest known individual: no information.

ⓘ General information

The waxwing gets its name from the unusual red tips on some of its secondaries, which, when examined closely, look like the red wax used for old manuscript seals. It is a rare visitor to Ireland with very small numbers seen in the east and north of the island in most winters. Occasionally large numbers migrate across Western Europe, many reaching Ireland, a phenomenon referred to as an invasion or irruption. These invasions occur when the berry crops fail on their normal wintering grounds in Eastern Europe and Russia following a better-than-usual breeding season the previous year. This forces many waxwings to move west in search of food. It is attracted to berries, especially rowan but also cotoneaster and pyracantha and others. If there is a large invasion a flock may descend on a garden and strip a berry bush in a day or two before moving on in search of their next meal.

Confusion species

None, but from a distance starlings (p. 164) have a similar shape and size in flight, and share the habit of flocking on wires, etc.

Wren *Troglodytes troglodytes*

Dreoilín

Length = 9–10cm
Wingspan = 14–15cm
All-Ireland population: 6.2 million individuals

Rank
12
Garden
Bird Survey

Seen in
78%
of gardens
in Ireland

Identification features

Smaller than a blue tit. A tiny, rusty-brown bird; paler below; pale supercilium; short rounded wings; fairly long, thin down-curved beak; long thin brown legs. Often cocks its tail so high it almost touches the back of its head. **In flight:** low straight buzzing flight.

Voice guide: The song is very loud, high and energetic. It has a variety of calls, the most noticeable being a loud short *tchic*, often repeated many times in an irregular, mechanical fashion. Cocks its tail when singing.

Diet: mainly insects and spiders.

Food to put out: Will occasionally eat breadcrumbs and small bits of cheese on the ground.

Nesting season: mid-April to mid-June.

Nest location: Nests in hollows or cavities in scrub and undergrowth, hedges, stone walls, cliffs, bogs, even old teapots and will occasionally use a blue-tit-type nest box.

Nest: ball-shaped, made of moss and leaves and has an entrance on the side. The nest is built by the male and lined by the female.

Eggs: five to seven, 17mm, occasionally as many as 16 shiny white eggs finely spotted with colours ranging from rusty brown to grey or black, often concentrated at the broad end.

Incubation period: 17 days, by the female.

Fledging time: 16 days, fed by both parents.

Number of broods reared per year: one.

Nest box: open-front or large-hole entrance box.

Average lifespan: two years

Oldest known individual: six years

Confusion species

Dunnock (p. 118) is larger, dark grey below, more frequently seen on the ground and has a longer tail which is never raised high in the air. Treecreeper (p. 152) is very white below and never raises its tail.

Ad.

Juv.

General information

A symbol of the dark and earth, the tradition of the 'wran' hunt (latterly on St Stephen's Day), dates back to Neolithic times. The third smallest bird in Europe after the goldcrest and firecrest, it would definitely qualify as one of the noisiest. Its Latin name means 'cave-dweller', which aptly describes its behaviour as it spends most of its time deep inside hedges, bushes and undergrowth. Being so small, wrens die in large numbers during very cold weather and indeed they are less common in more exposed areas of the west of the country during the winter months. With an average life span of less than two years, nature ensures its survival by providing many young. Wrens can be polygamous, with a male having two or three females with nests.

Dunnock *Prunella modularis*

Hedge Sparrow   Bráthair
an dreoilín/Dunnóg

Length = 14–15cm
Wingspan = 19–20cm
All-Ireland population: 1.7 million
individuals

Rank
11
Garden
Bird Survey

Seen in
79%
of gardens
in Ireland

Identification features

Similar in size to a robin. **Upperparts:** dark brown, streaked black;
no obvious wing markings. **Underside:** dark grey, paler toward
the undertail coverts; dark streaking on the flanks; eyes deep red
or brown; beak short, thin and black; legs long, thin and reddish-
brown. Juveniles boldly streaked on the underparts. When feeding,
hops along open ground, usually under bushes, hedgerows or bird
tables and feeders. **In flight:** slightly undulating but not very fast.
No noticeable features.

Voice guide: Call is a high thin *seeep*. The song is wren-like though
not as loud or as long.

Diet: mostly insects, in winter also seeds.
Food to put out: crushed peanuts, kitchen scraps and seed on the
ground.
Nesting season: April to mid-June.
Nest location: The nest is usually well hidden in bushes or under-
growth in a wide range of habitats from gardens to bracken-covered
hillsides.
Nest: a cup made of twigs and other plant material lined with moss,
hair or sometimes feathers. Built by both male and female.
Eggs: four to five, 20mm, shiny unmarked bright green-blue eggs, rarely
with fine red-brown spots.
Incubation period: 14 days, by the female.
Fledging time: 12–14 days, fed by both parents.
Number of broods reared per year: one to two.
Nest box: no.
Average lifespan: two years.
Oldest known individual: 11 years.

recently
fledged
Juv.

ⓘ General information

This unobtrusive little brown bird has a very complex social system and does not form pairs (as most birds do), but breeds in groups of up to three males and three females, with two males and a female being the most common. In the winter, hedges and ground flora are very important for both food and shelter. A largely sedentary bird, it rarely travels far. It is common, except in some parts of the north and extreme west.

Confusion species

Wren (p. 116) is much smaller, fast moving, pale brown undersides and has a short, stiff raised tail. Juvenile Robin (p. 120) can superficially resemble Dunnock. Treecreeper (p. 152) is white below and creeps up tree trunks and branches.

Robin *Erithacus rubecula*

Spideog

Length = 14cm
Wingspan = 20–21cm
All-Ireland population: 5.4 million individuals

Rank
1
Garden
Bird Survey

Seen in
99%
of gardens
in Ireland

Identification features

Adult: bright red-orange breast; grey-white belly; warm brown unmarked upperparts; grey on the side of the neck and upper breast; stands upright; round appearance. **Immature:** young birds just out of the nest do not have a red breast, but instead are scaled light and dark brown. **In flight:** flies fast and straight.

Voice guide: Its call is a loud, thin *tick*, usually repeated several times, often out of sight. It sings all year round but is at its loudest during spring, when its melodious twittering is often performed from a fence-post or a prominent bush, sometimes at night in suburban areas.

Diet: insects, especially beetles and their larvae, also fruit and seeds in winter.

Food to put out: seed cake, seeds, bread and will sometimes take peanuts.

Nesting season: mid-March to mid-June.

Nest location: a wide variety of places from trees and shrubs to ivy-covered walls and even ledges in sheds, etc.

Nest: a big cup nest made of dead leaves and other plant material, lined with thin roots, hair and, rarely, feathers. Built by the female.

Eggs: four to six, 20mm, matt white or cream eggs with red-brown markings ranging from fine flecks to blotches spread all over the eggs or concentrated towards the broad end of the eggs.

Incubation period: 14 days, by female.

Fledging time: 13–14 days, fed by both parents.

Number of broods reared per year: two.

Nest box: open-front box.

Average lifespan: two years.

Oldest known individual: eight years.

Juv.

Ad.

Juv.
moulting
to Ad.

General information

Probably the best-known bird species in Ireland, and also the 'friendliest'. In the breeding season robins are extremely territorial and will chase off any intruding birds. Occasionally, disputes between neighbouring birds can become very violent. Nests anywhere there is ground cover and will sometimes use garden sheds. It is a constant companion to the gardener, feeding on grubs, worms and insects disturbed by the fork or spade, and can become very tame. It is a widespread visitor to bird tables and increasingly to hanging feeders. BirdWatch Ireland's Countryside Bird Survey indicates a slight decrease in population in recent years.

Confusion species

Juvenile robins, which lack the red breast, may look similar to the dunnock (p. 118). Stonechat (p. 112) smaller but can superficially resemble adult and young robins.

Stonechat *Saxicola torquata*

Caislín dearg/Caislín cloch

J F M A M J J A S O N D

Length = 12–13cm
Wingspan = 19–20cm
All-Ireland population: 118,000 individuals

Rank
50+
Garden
Bird Survey

Seen in
<1%
of gardens
in Ireland

Identification features

Slightly smaller than a robin. **Male:** black head; white patches on the side of the neck and on the wings; bright orange breast and flanks; back streaked dark brown and black; creamy white rump; short black tail; legs long and black; in winter duller and paler. **Female:** paler brown version of the male; little or no white; less striking orange-brown breast, and lacks pale rump. Hops on the ground. **In flight:** straight, weak, buzzing flight; makes short flights to catch flies and pounces on insects on the ground from a prominent position.

Voice guide: It gets its name from its call which is a loud short *tchack-tchack* (like two stones being struck together), sometimes preceded by a longer thin *weeet* sound and accompanied by wing- and tail-flicking. The song is an unremarkable, often double-noted, twittering.

Diet: invertebrates, occasionally berries; hunts from perch, descending to pick up food from ground.

Food to put out: none.

Nesting season: end March to end June.

Nest Location: on or just above the ground in thick vegetation with a preference for areas of gorse and young forestry plantations.

Nest: cup-shaped; made of grass, moss and other plant material lined with hair, wool and, rarely, feathers. Nest built by the female.

Eggs: five to six, 19mm, slightly shiny pale green-blue eggs with fine red-brown flecks all over, sometimes concentrated near the broad end of the eggs.

Incubation period: 14–15 days, usually by female.

Fledging time: 13–15 days, fed by both parents.

Number of broods reared per year: two to three.

Nest box: no.

Average lifespan: no data available.

Oldest known individual: four years.

Juv.

F.

NBr. M.

Br. M.

F.

General information

The stonechat is a sedentary species. Most abundant along the west coast, it has declined in recent years due to intensive farming and increased human disturbance caused by recreational activities. This decline is most noticeable in the east and midlands. Retreats from higher ground in the winter and is mainly found along the coast. Very sensitive to cold weather when large numbers die, but, following a few mild winters and because of their ability to raise up to three broods of young in a season, their numbers soon recover. BirdWatch Ireland's Countryside Bird Survey indicates a decrease in population in recent years.

Confusion species

Females and young stonechats sometimes resemble young robins (p. 120).

Blackbird *Turdus merula*

Lon dubh

Length = 24–27cm
Wingspan = 35–36cm
All-Ireland population: 4.9 million individuals

Rank
2
Garden
Bird Survey

Seen in
99%
of gardens
in Ireland

Identification features

Male: jet-black body, short, heavy, bright orange-yellow beak and eye-ring. Young males superficially resemble female birds. **Female:** dark chocolate-brown, with paler throat and breast (sometimes faintly spotted); dark-brown beak; no eye-ring. Partial or total albino blackbirds are not unusual. **In flight:** over short distances, fast and straight flight. On landing will often droop its wings and cock its tail high in the air.

Voice guide: Sings from a high prominent position, from late January well into summer. The song is melodious and loud, sometimes continuing for a long period. Calls include a loud chock and a high-pitched, thin sseeee. If disturbed, flies away with a loud clamorous call. Unlike the similar-sounding song thrush it rarely repeats song phrases.

Diet: mainly insects and earthworms, also fruit and berries.

Food to put out: bread, seed cake, seed and fruit.

Nesting season: mid-March to mid-June.

Nest location: Will nest in a variety of sites, usually with trees, shrubs or hedges, preferring a fork in a tree or shrub.

Nest: a stout cup-shaped nest made from a variety of plant material, lined with a mixture of mud and plant material and finished with strands of dead grass. Built by the female.

Eggs: three to five, 29mm, shiny pale green-blue eggs covered in fine brown or rusty brown flecks and spots sometimes concentrated around the broad end of the egg.

Incubation period: 15 days, usually by the female.

Fledging time: 15 days, fed by both parents, and dependent on them for a further two or three weeks after fledging.

Number of broods reared per year: two to three.

Nest box: nest bundles, occasionally small platforms.

Average lifespan: three years.

Oldest known individual: 14 years.

Ad. F.

Ad. F.

Ad. M.

Juv.

Leucistic Male

 General information

Likes open, short grass and leaf litter when feeding. Blackbirds can often be observed looking and listening for earthworms that are on or just below the surface of the ground. If frightened on the ground it will sometimes lower its head and run quickly to the nearest cover. With nearly 2 million breeding pairs in Ireland, it is no wonder that it is so well known. It is common everywhere but was rare in the west in the 19th century. Its dark plumage and low-pitched voice has led researchers to believe that the blackbird was once a species mainly found in forests before human intervention altered the landscape in Europe by removing most of the forests. In winter, many blackbirds from Britain and Scandinavia join our mainly resident birds.

Confusion species

Starling (p. 164) is smaller, usually covered in pale spots; has pale pink/red legs and short tail.

Fieldfare *Turdus pilaris*

Sacán/Glaisneach

Length = 25–27cm
Wingspan = 39–41cm
Winter population: no data

Rank
36
Garden
Bird Survey

Seen in
9%
of gardens
in Ireland

Identification features

About the same size as a blackbird. Unlike the other thrushes that might visit your garden it has a dark tail and contrasting pale grey rump and lower back. The nape and crown are also grey. Breast yellow-tan with dark streaks, flanks heavily spotted, yellow-or-ange beak with a dark tip, duller on young birds, legs long and dark. When perched fieldfares will often hold their wings slightly drooped. **In flight:** They fly straight and the combination of the dark tail, grey rump and lower back and white patches on the inner underwing are unique.

Voice guide: A loud mechanical *tchak-tchak-tchak* most often heard in flight.

Diet: Insects and worms and in winter will also eat berries and other fruit.

Food to put out: Apples and seed on the ground.

Nesting Season: Not recorded as a breeding species in Ireland. Breeds from late April to mid-June in woodland and parkland in northern Europe and Russia.

Nest: a cup-shaped nest made from a variety of plant materials, lined with mud and then some thin strands of grass. Built by the female.

Eggs: five to six, 29mm, shiny light blue or pale grey or pale olive eggs covered with fine red-brown flecks.

Incubation period: 13–15 days.

Fledging time: 12–16 days.

Number of broods reared per year: one to two.

Average lifespan: no data available.

Oldest known individual: 14 years.

Confusion species
None.

General information

The fieldfare is usually seen in Ireland during cold winter months. Usually encountered in flocks, often in association with redwings though never as numerous. Its name comes from old Anglo-Saxon meaning 'the traveller over the fields'. With our winters becoming milder in recent years fieldfares are not seen as often as before. During hard weather they will occasionally enter gardens and orchards to feed on windfall fruit and berry bushes.

Song Thrush *Turdus philomelos*

Smólach ceoil/Smólach

Length = 21–23cm
Wingspan = 33–34cm
All-Ireland population: 956,000 individuals

Rank
14
Garden
Bird Survey

Seen in
72%
of gardens
in Ireland

Identification features

Slightly smaller and slimmer than a blackbird. **Upperparts:** plain, warm brown; **underside:** pale buff with conspicuous black spots, arranged so close together as to form lines, thinnest on the throat and upper breast, thickest with largest spots on the flanks and belly; eyes black; beak small and sharp, looks up-tilted; legs long and pink. On open ground often makes short dashes. **In flight:** Mainly unmarked upper parts, pale buff-orange inner underwing.

Voice guide: Its call is a loud *thick*, repeated several times quickly. The song, delivered from a high leafy perch, roof or TV aerial, is similar to that of a blackbird, but more musical and structured, containing short phrases repeated clearly, usually two to four times.

Diet: mainly earthworms and insects. During dry periods will eat snails and in the autumn and winter will eat berries and other fruit also.

Food to put out: May take fruit and kitchen scraps from the ground.

Nesting season: mid-March to mid-June.

Nest location: Usually nests in a well-hidden site in trees or shrubs and occasionally on buildings.

Nest: a neat cup-shaped nest made of a variety of plant materials lined with mud or rotten wood pulp. Nest built by the female.

Eggs: four to six, 27mm, slightly shiny bright pale green-blue eggs with flecks or spots ranging in colour from dark green to dark rusty red. Usually only a light scattering of marks, rarely concentrated towards the broad end of the egg.

Incubation period: 12–14 days, by female.

Fledging time: 13–15 days, fed by both parents.

Number of broods reared per year: two to three.

Nest box: nest bundles and occasionally small platforms.

Average Lifespan: three years.

Oldest known individual: ten years.

Juv.

Ad.

General information

Like other thrushes, the song thrush likes earthworms and can be seen feeding on large lawns and parks. It also likes snails, which it smashes open on a small rock or tree stump, often referred to as an anvil, leaving a large number of broken shells scattered about. In Britain, an alarming increase in the use of snail-killing chemicals in recent years, both commercially and domestically, is thought to be the main cause of a recent decline there. Like the blackbird, song thrushes from Britain and Scandinavia come here each winter and in severe cold winters thrushes from all over the continent arrive here in large numbers. BirdWatch Ireland's Countryside Bird Survey indicates a slight decrease in population in recent years.

Confusion species

Redwing (p. 130) a winter visitor, is slightly smaller; pale buff super-cilium; dark red-orange on inner underwings and flanks; call a thin *tseeep*. Mistle thrush (p. 132) is larger; colder brown; white inner underwing; round spots not arranged in lines; stands very upright.

Redwing *Turdus iliacus*

Deargán sneachta

J F M A M J J A S O N D

Length = 20–22cm
Wingspan = 33–35cm
Winter population: no data

Rank
31
Garden
Bird Survey

Seen in
11%
of gardens
in Ireland

Identification features

Smaller than a blackbird. Rusty red flanks and inner underwing, large cream supercilium, white breast and belly with dark streaking on the breast and flanks. **In flight:** flies straight, usually not alone. Inner part of the underwing dark rusty red, unlike that of the song thrush which is mid-brown.

Voice guide: The call is a distinctive high wheezing *tzeeee*, often heard from migrating birds passing overhead at night, in late autumn and winter.

Diet: Insects, also berries in autumn and winter.

Food to put out: apples on the ground.

Nesting season: Breeds from late April to end June in a variety of habitats from woodlands to gardens in Iceland, northern Europe and Russia. Has never been recorded breeding in Ireland.

Nest: a cup-shaped nest made from a variety of plant materials, sometimes lined with mud and then thin strands of grass. Built by the female.

Eggs: four to six, 26mm, shiny pale blue or green-blue or grey eggs covered with fine flecks of red-brown.

Incubation period: 12–15 days, usually by the female.

Fledging time: 11–15 days.

Number of broods reared per year: two.

Average lifespan: no data available.

Oldest known individual: 12 years.

Confusion species

Song thrush (p. 128) and mistle thrush (p. 132) lack the rusty red colour on the flanks and inner underwing and do not have a pale supercilium.

ⓘ **General information**

The redwing is a winter visitor to Ireland. Rarely seen alone, they often form flocks of hundreds and sometimes thousands of individuals. The less numerous fieldfare often joins these flocks. The redwing migrates from its breeding grounds in Iceland and northern Europe and can be heard at night flying overhead in late autumn and winter. The Irish name for this bird, deargán sneachta – which means 'the red one of the snow' – shows that in Ireland it was associated with cold weather and indeed during very harsh winter weather large numbers fly to Ireland to escape freezing weather conditions on the continent.

Mistle Thrush *Turdus viscivorus*

Smólach mór/Liatráisc

J F M A M J J A S O N D

Length = 27cm
Wingspan = 44–45cm
All-Ireland population: 242,000 individuals

Rank
26
Garden
Bird Survey

Seen in
28%
of gardens
in Ireland

Identification features

Larger than a blackbird. On the ground it stands very erect and looks pot-bellied. **Upperparts:** dusty grey-brown; wing feathers pale fringed; pale outer tail feathers, palest at the tips. **Underside:** white with fine streaks and blotches on the throat and breast; belly has large distinct dark spots, not forming lines. **In flight:** white inner underwing; very undulating flight, a series of wing flaps and glides with wings closed.

Voice guide: Call is a distinctive rapid, harsh chattering *tuck-tuck-tuck,* often heard when in flight. Its song is similar to that of a blackbird but less musical and more repetitive, often delivered from a high perch, even in winter.

Diet: insects, worms and also berries in autumn and winter.
Food to put out: May take bread and apples.
Nesting season: mid-March to late May.
Nest location: usually in the fork of a tree in an open area, not usually hidden.
Nest: a large cup-shaped nest made of a variety of plant materials and some mud, lined with fine grass. Built by the female.
Eggs: three to five, 31mm, shiny eggs, ranging in colour from pale green-blue to pale cream-red with flecks, spots or blotches of rusty brown or purple-grey.
Incubation period: 13–16 days, by the female.
Fledging time: 13–15 days, fed by both parents.
Number of broods reared per year: two to three.
Nest box: no.
Average lifespan: three years.
Oldest known individual: 11 years.

Confusion species

Song thrush (p. 128) is much smaller, with warmer colours; light brown inner underwing, does not look so spotted.

Juv.

Ad.

Ad.

General information

The mistle thrush breeds in all parts of Ireland, though scarcer on the south coast, particularly in County Cork. Unknown in Ireland until 1800 when one was shot in County Antrim. By the end of the 19th century it was breeding in every county. The reasons for this colonisation are unknown. In the breeding season it feeds its young mainly on caterpillars and flies. In the winter it defends a feeding territory, especially a berry bush or tree, with a particular fondness for holly trees. On the continent it defends large areas of mistletoe, from which it gets its name. Less migratory than other thrushes, our own birds are sedentary and are joined by small numbers from Britain in the winter. Forms loose, roving family flocks in late summer. BirdWatch Ireland's Countryside Bird Survey indicates a decrease in population in recent years.

Blackcap *Sylvia atricapilla*

Caipín dubh

J F M A M J J A S O N D

Length = 14cm
Wingspan = 21–22cm
All-Ireland population: 267,000 individuals

Rank
21
Garden
Bird Survey

Seen in
49%
of gardens
in Ireland

Identification features

Same size as a robin. **Male:** neat, jet-black cap; cold brown-grey upperparts; pale throat and undertail. **Female:** less distinctive, pale, chestnut-brown cap, slightly browner overall.

Voice guide: The call is a harsh *tcek* repeated many times if alarmed. The song is a series of very varied warbling notes, becoming louder towards the end.

Diet: insects in the summer, otherwise seed, berries and fruit.
Food to put out: seed cake, seed, peanuts and fruit.
Nesting season: late April to mid-June.
Nest location: open deciduous, coniferous or mixed woodland with bushes and undergrowth.
Nest: a small neat cup-shaped nest made of a variety of plant materials, occasionally with wool and hair and lined with fine grass and hair. Built by both female and male.
Eggs: four to six, 20mm, shiny, unevenly coloured cream eggs sometimes with a tint of red with a few spots, flecks or scribbles of dark brown.
Incubation period: 12–14 days, by female and male.
Fledging time: 10–13 days, fed by both parents.
Number of broods reared per year: one to two.
Nest box: no.
Average lifespan: two years.
Oldest known individual: ten years.

Confusion species

None.

F.

F.

M.

M.

ⓘ General information

Mainly a summer visitor from Africa to deciduous woodlands, where it can be difficult to see, but the jaunty song is notable. Over the last 25 years blackcaps have been overwintering in Ireland in increasing numbers. These individuals come here from a separate continental European breeding population. In winter, areas of ivy with berries are worth checking for this neat bird as are cordyline trees, where the fruiting bracts are similarly attractive. When visiting bird tables, for apples or peanuts, it can behave quite aggressively, chasing other birds away. BirdWatch Ireland's Countryside Bird Survey indicates a large increase in population in recent years.

Chiffchaff *Phylloscopus collybita*

Tiuf-teaf

| J | F | M | A | M | J | J | A | S | O | N | D |

Length = 11cm
Wingspan = 17–18cm
All-Ireland population: 296,000 individuals

Recorded in
44%
of squares in the Countryside Bird Survey

Identification features

Slightly bigger than a wren. **Upperparts:** pale green-grey. **Underside:** very light yellow-grey; thin dark eye-stripe; narrow, pale, supercilium; legs and beak dark grey-black. **In flight:** weak, slightly undulating flight; moves busily from branch to branch in search of insects on leaves, flicking wings and tail. This and the very similar willow warbler are very difficult to distinguish from each other, except by their songs.

Voice guide: It gets its name from its song, which cannot be confused with any other species in Ireland. It is a loud strident bouncing *chiff-chaff-chiff-chiff-chaff* lasting five or more seconds at a time. Usually heard before the willow warbler arrives in mid-April, with overwintering birds singing as early as the beginning of March. The singing bird is often difficult to locate as it is hidden by foliage at the top of the tree canopy. Its contact call is a soft *wheeet*.

Diet: insects, some fruit in autumn and winter.
Food to put out: none.
Nesting season: mid-April to mid-June.
Nest location: Likes to build on or very close to the ground in thick undergrowth in woodland and hedgerows.
Nest: Made of a variety of plant materials, with a dome on it and lined with feathers. Built by the female.
Eggs: four to six, 15mm, shiny white eggs with a light scattering of flecks and spots ranging from dark purple to dark brown.
Incubation period: 13–14 days, by the female.
Fledging time: 13–15 days, fed mainly by the female.
Number of broods reared per year: one to two.
Nest box: no.
Average lifespan: two years.
Oldest known individual: seven years.

Juv.

Ad.
(autumn)

Ad.
(spring)

ℹ️ General information

A common summer visitor with a slightly thinner distribution in treeless areas of the west and at higher altitudes. Not found very far from deciduous trees. Most winter south of the Sahara desert but some overwinter here. The chiffchaff was quite scarce in Ireland in the 19th century, with the population increasing steadily in the first quarter of the 20th century. During autumn migration, chiffchaffs from Scandinavia and western Russia have been identified in Ireland. BirdWatch Ireland's Countryside Bird Survey indicates a slight increase in population in recent years.

Confusion species

Willow warbler (p. 138) is similar in size, shape and pattern but paler and less yellow-looking; usually has distinctive pale legs. Only reliably separated by their song. Goldcrest (p. 140) has pale wing bars and crown stripe.

Willow Warbler *Phylloscopus trochilus*

Ceolaire sailí

`J F M A M J J A S O N D`

Length = 11–12cm
Wingspan = 18–19cm
All-Ireland population: 1.665 million
individuals

Recorded in
72%
of squares in the
Countryside Bird Survey

Identification features

Slightly bigger than a wren. Similar in size, shape and pattern to the chiffchaff, but brighter and more yellow looking, usually has pale legs. Very difficult to distinguish from the chiffchaff except by its song. **Upperparts:** pale green-grey. **Underside:** thin dark eye-stripe; narrow, pale supercilium; very light cream breast, white belly; legs usually pale. **In flight:** weak, slightly undulating flight; moves busily from branch to branch in search of insects on leaves; flicks wings and tail.

Voice guide: Its song is a loud, clear, cascading warble, quiet and slow at the start, louder and faster at the end, lasting three or four seconds. Call is a soft short *woo-eet*, similar to chiffchaff.

Diet: insects and spiders, also berries in the autumn.

Food to put out: none.

Nesting season: late April to early June.

Nest location: Usually found on the ground under the cover of shrubs, undergrowth and trees with low branches, often in open woodland.

Nest: small nest made from a variety of plant materials; has a dome and is usually lined with feathers. Built by the female.

Eggs: five to seven, 15mm, shiny white or pale cream eggs with a light scattering of light red-brown flecks spots or blotches.

Incubation period: 13–15 days, by the female.

Fledging time: 13–16 days, fed by both parents.

Number of broods reared per year: one to two.

Nest box: no.

Average lifespan: two years.

Oldest known individual: 11 years.

Confusion species

Chiffchaff (p. 136) is similar in size, shape and pattern but slightly duller and more yellow-looking; usually has dark legs. Only reliably separated by their song. Goldcrest (p. 140) has pale wing bars and crown stripe.

Juv.

Ad.

1st W.

Ad.

General information

Far more common than the chiffchaff and indeed, with at least 800,000 breeding pairs in Ireland, the willow warbler is our most common summer visitor. It arrives later than the chiffchaff, usually in April, and departs earlier. It occupies a wider range of habitats, broadly favouring willow and birch scrub. BirdWatch Ireland's Countryside Bird Survey indicates a slight increase in population in recent years.

Goldcrest *Regulus regulus*

Cíorbhuí/Dreoilín easpaig J F M A M J J A S O N D

Length = 9cm
Wingspan = 13–14cm
All-Ireland population: 721,500
individuals

Rank
27
Garden
Bird Survey

Seen in
26%
of gardens
in Ireland

Identification features

Tiny, smaller than a wren. Large head with a stripe on the centre of
the crown, orange on the male and yellow on the female, bordered
by black; gives the bird its name. **Adult:** olive green above and pale
grey below. Wings are dark brown with pale edges to both primaries and secondaries forming a pale panel on the closed wing;
noticeable buff wing bar; very short, thin black beak; pink-brown
legs. Black eye looks relatively large, a feature accentuated by a
broad pale area around the eye. **Immature:** young birds lack the
crown stripe. **In flight:** weak, slightly undulating flight, rapid wing
beats. Flits from branch to branch and often hovers while catching
insects on leaves.

Voice guide: Its call, usually heard before the bird is seen, is a very
thin, high-pitched, erratic *szitt-szitt-szitt*. Its song is also very high-
pitched and includes a rapid *fh-he-hee*, usually repeated four times,
followed by a similar more varied phrase.

Diet: Insects, especially greenfly, caterpillars and also spiders.
Food to put out: May take seed cake, fat or grated cheese.
Nesting season: mid-April to mid-June.
Nest location: Prefers coniferous woodland, but also mixed wood-
land, parks and gardens with coniferous trees or bushes.
Nest: a small cup-shaped nest, which hangs from a branch. The nest
is built from mosses and lichens and held together by spiders' webs.
Usually lined with feathers. Built by the female and the male.
Eggs: six to nine, 14mm, matt cream or pale brown eggs covered with
fine red-brown flecks often concentrated near the broad end of the
egg.
Incubation period: 15–17 days, by the female.
Fledging time: 17–17 days, fed by both parents.
Number of broods reared per year: two.
Nest box: no.
Average lifespan: two years.
Oldest known individual: four years.

rest flat

crest raised

Juv.

M.

ⓘ General information

The goldcrest is the smallest bird in Europe and weighs just 6g. It feeds on insects, which it catches by inspecting what appears to be every inch of every leaf it comes across. In summer it raises two broods, starting the second when the first is only half-grown, and laying eggs adding up to almost twice its body weight in one brood. In winter, goldcrests from Britain and northern Europe join our own, and noticeable decreases in its population are recorded following severe winters. Goldcrests sometimes join roving flocks of tit species in winter. BirdWatch Ireland's Countryside Bird Survey indicates a slight decrease in population in recent years.

Confusion species

Willow warbler (p. 138) and chiffchaff (p. 136) are similar in size and appearance but lack markings on the head and do not have wing bars.

Spotted Flycatcher *Muscicapa striata*

Cuilsealgaire

J F M A M J J A S O N D

Length = 14cm
Wingspan = 23–24cm
All-Ireland population: 41,000 individuals

Recorded in
10%
of squares in the
Countryside Bird Survey

Identification features

About the size of a robin. The name is a bit of a misnomer as the adult birds are streaked rather than spotted. Rather a plain-looking bird. **Upperparts:** the crown, which is peaked at the rear, is closely streaked grey-white and dark brown. **Underside:** throat, breast and belly very pale grey-brown; dark streaks on breast and flanks; undertail coverts white; wings dark grey-brown, faint wing bar; back slightly paler. Usually seen alone, sitting erect on an exposed branch in readiness to swoop for insect prey. **In flight:** darts out from a perch on a branch with a broad, agile sweep to catch an insect in mid-air, returning to the same position or a nearby branch. **Voice guide:** Makes a low harsh *tsee* call and an unremarkable subtle song.

Diet: mainly flying insects.

Food to put out: none.

Nesting season: mid-May to mid-July.

Nest location: Breeds in a variety of habitats with trees. The nest is usually located next to a tree trunk, behind dead bark, in holes in trees, walls or crevices.

Nest: a cup-shaped nest made of a variety of plant materials and spiders' webs. Lined with feathers, hair and dead leaves. Built by the female with some help from the male.

Eggs: four to five, 19mm, matt cream to pale blue-green eggs with flecks, spots and blotches of red-brown to purple-red sometimes concentrated near the broad end of the egg.

Incubation period: 12–14 days, by female only.

Fledging time: 13–15 days; the parents feed the young for up to three weeks after they leave the nest.

Number of broods reared per year: one to two.

Nest box: open-fronted box.

Average lifespan: two years.

Oldest known individual: eight years.

Confusion species

None.

Ad.

Ad.

Juv.

ℹ️ General information

A thinly distributed summer visitor to deciduous woodland and rural villages, farm buildings and parkland. The spotted flycatcher is one of the last of our summer visitors to arrive, usually in the first week of May, and very susceptible to cold, wet weather during the breeding season. It has declined in recent years. Weather conditions, both here and on its way south to its wintering grounds in southern Africa, are thought to be a major factor. Not as common in the west, away from deciduous trees or at higher altitudes.

Long-tailed Tit *Aegithalos caudatus*

Meantán earrfhada

J F M A M J J A S O N D

Length = 12–14cm
Wingspan = 17–18cm
All-Ireland population: 115,600
individuals

Rank
23
Garden
Bird Survey

Seen in
47%
of gardens
in Ireland

Identification features

Smaller than a robin. Out-sized black and white tail, as long as its small, dull-pink, black and white body. **Upperparts:** head grey-white with broad black stripe above the eye; back and wings black with pink patches at the base of the wings; pale edges to the second-aries. **Underside:** throat and breast dirty white, becoming grey-pink on the belly and undertail; orange-red eye rings; black eyes and legs; tiny beak. **In flight:** reluctant to fly even short distances. Weak, slightly undulating flight. Usually seen in shrub or tree canopy, forming restless feeding flocks, ranging in size from three or four to over 20 birds.

Voice guide: Flocks in winter can be quite noisy, making a variety of calls, including a short low *chrup* and a faster thin *ssee-ssee-ssee*. Its song is similar to its call notes.

Diet: mainly small insects, caterpillars, spiders, including larvae and eggs. Food to put out: seedcake, seed and peanuts.

Nesting season: late March to late April.

Nest location: Breeds in woodland areas with a preference for dense undergrowth. Also nests in thick hedgerows and in trees.

Nest: nest resembles an elongated ball, containing sometimes up to 2,000 feathers, held together by spiders' webs, and very well camou-flaged by a covering of lichens. Nest built by both the female and male.

Eggs: six to eight, 14 mm, shiny white or pale cream eggs with variable red-brown flecks and spots ranging from just a few to covering the egg and sometimes concentrated towards the broad end.

Incubation period: 13–16 days, mainly by the female.

Fledging time: 15–17 days, fed by both parents.

Number of broods reared per year: one.

Nest box: no.

Average lifespan: two years.

Oldest known individual: eight years.

Confusion species
None.

Ad.

Juv.

ℹ️ General information

During winter nights a long-tailed tit flock, which is comprised of family members and relatives, will huddle close together for warmth. During the winter days it remains with the flock, which helps it to find food more successfully and so survive the winter. In spring the flock breaks up and each pair sets up a territory.

Coal Tit *Parus ater*

Meantán dubh

Length = 11–12cm
Wingspan = 18–19cm
All-Ireland population: 925,000 individuals

Rank
6
Garden
Bird Survey

Seen in
94%
of gardens
in Ireland

Identification features

Smaller than a robin. **Upperparts:** Long white patch on the nape; black head and white ear coverts; dark wings with two faint white wing bars; dark grey-brown back and tail. **Underside:** pale buff-grey; beak short and thin; legs long and dark blue-grey. Comes readily to bird tables and has a mischievous jizz. Dull in colour compared to the other tits. **In flight:** weak, bouncing flight, short bursts of rapid wing beats.

Voice guide: Its calls and song are varied but include a high, forced fee-chew repeated several times; also a very high, goldcrest-like *su-ee-ou, zit-zit-zit, suee-ou.*

Diet: insect and spiders, also seeds in winter.

Food to put out: seed cake, seed and peanuts.

Nesting season: late April and May.

Nest location: Prefers conifer trees but will also nest in broadleaved trees. Usually nests in a hole, sometimes in walls.

Nest: a cup-shaped nest made from a variety of plant materials and spiders' webs and lined with hair, delicate plant material and feathers. Built by the female.

Eggs: eight to ten, 16mm, slightly shiny white or pale cream eggs with scattered red-brown blotches and flecks, usually darker than those of blue tit.

Incubation period: 14–17 days by the female.

Fledging time: 16–19 days, fed by both parents.

Number of broods reared per year: one to two.

Nest box: hole-entrance box.

Average lifespan: two years.

Oldest known individual: eight years.

Confusion species

Blue tit (p. 148) and great tit (p. 150) are both more colourful and lack the distinctive white stripe on the nape.

Juv.

Ad.

General information

The coal tit is fond of wooded areas, with a particular prefer-ence for conifers and also sessile oak and birch. It is widespread in Ireland, absent only from treeless areas, particularly in the extreme west. Resident, rarely travelling far. In winter, it often forms part of a flock consisting of different members of the tit family. Unlike other members of the tit family, however, it hoards food at any time of the year and so does not suffer so much in severe weather. In one incident, a birdwatcher put out 250g of whole peanuts on a bird table only to find that a coal tit had removed the lot in less than an hour, hiding the nuts in cracks in a nearby wall. BirdWatch Ireland's Countryside Bird Survey indicates a slight increase in population in recent years.

Blue Tit *Parus caeruleus*

Meantán gorm

J F M A M J J A S O N D

Rank
3
Garden
Bird Survey

Seen in
98%
of gardens
in Ireland

Length = 11–12cm
Wingspan = 17–18cm
All-Ireland population: 2.3 million
individuals

Identification features

Smaller than a robin. **Upperparts:** pale blue cap surrounded by a white halo; white ear coverts; dark line through the eye; back green-blue; wings blue with faint white wing bar; tail also blue. Underside: throat, side of the neck and nape dark blue; breast and belly pale yellow. **Immature:** similar in pattern to adults but more yellow in overall colour. **In flight:** weak, bouncing flight, rapid wing beats.

Voice guide: Like most members of the tit family, the blue tit is very vocal and has various call notes. The most characteristic are a very high *pfit-pfit-che-haah-ah* and a lower, scolding *churr*.

Diet: insect and spiders, also berries, fruit and seeds in winter.

Food to put out: Blue tits have a wide taste and especially like peanuts, seed cake, seeds and fat but will also check out almost any food put out to attract birds.

Nesting season: mid-April to mid-May.

Nest location: Nests in a wide variety of habitats from woodlands to gardens. The nest can be found in any suitable crevice or hollow in trees or walls. Regularly uses nest boxes.

Nest: a cup-shaped nest built mainly of moss and a variety of plant materials, lined with down and feathers. Built by the female.

Eggs: seven to eleven, 16mm, slightly shiny white eggs with fine red-brown to purple-red flecks, sometimes concen-trated at the broad end of the egg.

Incubation period: 13–15 days by the female, fed by the male.

Fledging time: 18–21 days, fed by both parents.

Number of broods reared per year: one.

Nest box: hole-entrance box.

Average lifespan: three years.

Oldest known individual: nine years.

Confusion species

Great tit (p. 150) and coal tit (p. 146) have black crowns.

Ad.

Ad.

Ad.

Juv.

Ad.

ⓘ General information

Ringing studies have shown that in the course of a winter's day, what you thought were three or four birds visiting your bird feeder may actually have been many more. Over an average winter period you might unwittingly have played host to hundreds of different blue tits! The blue tit rarely travels far, but there is an exception to every rule and one individual, ringed on Bardsey Island in Britain on 4 October 2003 was re-trapped alive and well 345km to the west on Cape Clear Island 19 days later.

Like all members of this family, the blue tit is very acrobatic and because it likes nesting in cracks in walls and trees it will usually take up residence in a nest box in no time at all. Like all birds, blue tits can see ultraviolet light. The front of their heads glows brightly under UV light; it is thought by some that females choose their partners based on the UV brightness of their heads!

Great Tit *Parus major*

Meantán mór

Length = 14cm
Wingspan = 23–24cm
All-Ireland population: 1.37 million individuals

Rank
4
Garden
Bird Survey

Seen in
96%
of gardens
in Ireland

Identification features

The largest member of the tit family. About the same size as a robin. **Upperparts:** jet-black head with bright white cheeks (ear coverts); dark blue-green primaries and secondaries, white wing bar; yellow-green back; tail feathers dark with varying degrees of pale blue edging; outer tail feather white (most noticeable from below). **Underside:** breast and belly bright yellow with a black line down the centre. The black line is broad on males and narrow and incomplete on females. White undertail coverts. Dark grey beak and pale blue-grey legs. **Immature:** plumage looks paler and less yellow.

Voice guide: When it comes to calls it is hard to beat the repertoire of the great tit. Calls and song include a blue tit-like *tchurrr* and distinct phrases usually repeated two to four times, one sounding like '*teacher, teacher!*' More mechanical and repetitive than blue tit or coal tit.

Diet: insects and spiders; in winter, beechmast, seeds, berries and fruit.
Food to put out: peanuts, seed cake, seed.
Nesting season: mid-April to mid-May.
Nest location: in a variety of habitats; usually nests in a hole or cavity in a tree or wall, and occasionally in very dense vegetation.
Nest: a cup-shaped nest made of a variety of plant materials, lined with thin strands of grass or feathers. Built by the female.
Eggs: seven to nine, 18mm, slightly shiny white or pale cream eggs with red-brown or light brown spots and flecks of variable size and density.
Incubation period: 13–15 days by the female, fed by the male.
Fledging time: 18–21 days, fed by both parents.
Number of broods reared per year: one.
Nest box: hole-entrance box.
Average lifespan: three years.
Oldest known individual: 14 years.

Ad. M.

Ad. F.

Ad. M.

Juv.

ℹ **General information**

The black stripe on the belly of a male great tit is an indicator of its status; it is thought that larger stripes are more attractive to females. As widespread as the blue tit, though not as numerous. Like other members of the tit family, the great tit is mostly sedentary, though there is evidence of continental birds arriving here in autumn. Because it is bigger and less acrobatic than its relatives, it spends more time looking for food on the ground. Favours beechmast and if there is a good crop will remain in woods later into autumn and winter. In bad beechmast years, it moves out of the woods in search of food sooner and turns up at bird tables earlier, where it is the dominant tit species. BirdWatch Ireland's Countryside Bird Survey indicates a slight increase in population in recent years.

Confusion species

Coal tit (p. 146) is smaller and has a white stripe down the nape and buff undersides. Blue tit (p. 148) has a bright blue cap.

Treecreeper *Certhia familiaris*

Meanglán/Snag

J F M A M J J A S O N D

Length = 12–13cm
Wingspan = 19cm
All-Ireland population: 82,300 individuals

Rank
38
Garden Bird Survey

Seen in
7%
of gardens in Ireland

Identification features

Thin curved beak, head and back dark brown with buff flecks; white eye stripe, dark wing feathers with buff edges and a buff wing bar. Rump and tail light tan. Tail long and stiff, with pointed tail feathers appearing as a fork when closed. Underside white. **In flight:** from above buff and dark wing bar, curved beak and long forked tail, from below gleaming white body. Undulating flight between trees with short bursts of wing beats. Rarely seen flying in the open.

Voice guide: The call of the treecreeper is a quiet high-pitched *zeee*, not unlike a goldcrest or a slightly louder *tchew* repeated several times in a row. The song is a complex mix of high descending notes starting with a short thrill.

Diet: insects, spiders, etc.

Food to put out: On rare occasions will take seed or nuts from bird tables.

Nesting season: April and May.

Nest location: Mainly deciduous woodland and parkland where there are suitable nest sites. Usually builds nest behind loose bark on a tree or behind ivy.

Nest: cup-shaped, made from small twigs and fine vegetable matter such as moss, dead grass and roots and lined with feathers, wool, and hair. Nest built by both the female and male.

Eggs: five to seven, 15–16mm, matt white with reddish-brown flecks which vary in intensity and are often concentrated at the broad end of the egg.

Incubation period: 13–16 days by the female while being fed by the male.

Fledging time: 15–17 days, fed by male at first while female broods the chicks, then by both parents.

Number of broods reared per year: one to two.

Nest box: special treecreeper box and occasionally hole-entrance box. See p. 45.

Average lifespan: two to three years.

Oldest known individual: nine years.

ℹ️ General information

The treecreeper is usually associated with large trees with rough bark such as oaks where it hunts for insects and larvae in the crevices and cracks. A unique bird, well camouflaged against the bark of a tree. It invariably climbs up trees, using its stiff tail as support; from a distance it may look like a mouse creeping up a tree. Sometimes associates with roaming tit flocks in winter. It roosts in a depression on a tree trunk and the site is usually marked with streaks of pale droppings.

Confusion species

The wren (p. 116) when viewed from behind can sometimes look and behave like a treecreeper but is grey-brown below and regularly raises its tail. Dunnock (p. 118) dull below, straight beak.

Jay *Garrulus glandarius*

Scréachóg choille

Length = 33–35cm
Wingspan = 54–56cm
All-Ireland population: 10,000 breeding pairs

Rank
35
Garden
Bird Survey

Seen in
10%
of gardens
in Ireland

Identification features

The most colourful of our crows, about the same size as a jackdaw. **Upperparts:** Finely streaked pale blue and black patches on the leading edge of the wing. White patches on black secondaries, white rump and dark tail. **Underside:** pink-brown body with white throat and undertail. **In flight:** only large woodland bird with large white rump.

Voice guide: Can be very noisy. The call is a loud raucous *kchaack* repeated at varying intervals, often delivered from deep cover.

Diet: caterpillars, beetles and other insects. In the autumn and winter will also eat fruit and seeds. Famous for hiding acorns.

Food to put out: fruit, seed cake; will occasionally take peanuts from feeders.

Nesting season: March and April.

Nest location: woodland and parkland habitats. The nest is usually built against the trunk or in a fork in a tree.

Nest: a cup-shaped nest made of twigs and some earth lined with light plant material and hair.

Eggs: four to six, 31mm, slightly shiny eggs ranging from pale blue-green to pale olive covered with fine flecks of light brown, grey or green and often scribbles towards the broad end.

Incubation period: 16–18 days by both parents.

Fledging time: 20–24 days. Fed initially by the male and then by both parents.

Number of broods reared per year: one.

Nest box: no.

Average lifespan: no data available.

Oldest known individual: 16 years.

Confusion species
None.

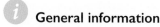

General information

The jay in Ireland is a separate race from that elsewhere in Europe, being noticeably darker and browner. Records show that the jay was very scarce in Ireland at the beginning of the 19th century, largely attributed to destruction of habitat and hunting. The bird was hunted mainly for its beautiful blue wing feathers, which are used to make fly hooks for fishing. Since the beginning of the 20th century the jay has expanded its range and is now found in and around deciduous and coniferous woodlands in most parts of the country, though it is nowhere very common.

Magpie *Pica pica*

Snag breac

Length = 44–48cm
Wingspan = 55–56cm
All-Ireland population: 755,500 individuals

Rank
7
Garden
Bird Survey

Seen in
91%
of gardens
in Ireland

Identification features

Upperparts: blue-green sheen on the black feathers, white 'braces' at the base of the wings and white on the primaries; black, wedge-ended tail as long as its body. **Underside:** head, throat and breast completely black; belly and flanks white; legs and beak black. **In flight:** long tail; blunt, rounded wings; black and white plumage.

Voice guide: Call is a harsh mechanical *chakk-kackk-kackk*. Song is more musical with high squeaks. Noisy when alarmed, especially near the nest, for example, by a nearby cat or bird of prey.

Diet: very varied, ranging from insects, seeds and fruit to carrion, kitchen scraps, eggs and nestlings.

Food to put out: seed cake, kitchen scraps; dog and cat food.

Nesting season: early April to early May.

Nest location: Nests in a variety of habitats where medium to tall trees are present. Utilises electricity poles and lamp posts in suburban areas.

Nest: a large nest, visible near the top of a tree before the leaves emerge. The nest is cup-shaped, made of twigs and some mud, lined with finer plant material and sometimes hair. Usually the nest is covered with a loose dome of twigs. The male usually brings the nest material and the female does the building.

Eggs: five to seven, 35mm, shiny eggs of varying shades of pale blue-green covered with small flecks and spots of dark brown or grey.

Incubation period: 18–20 days, by the female.

Fledging time: 26–31 days, fed by both parents.

Number of broods reared per year: one.

Nest box: no.

Average Lifespan: five years.

Oldest known individual: 21 years.

Confusion species
None.

General information

It might be hard to believe but up to the end of the 17th century magpies were unheard of in Ireland. Since then, they have spread to every corner of the island, but are most numerous in the east. In autumn, large flocks can be seen, sometimes over a hundred together. The magpie's ability to eat a wide variety of food, from insects and fruit to carrion, has made it a very successful species. One of the biggest myths relating to birds is that magpies are decimating our small-bird population. It is true that they will eat eggs and young of other birds, but many exhaustive studies have revealed that these food items comprise a very small part of their diet. Just because the magpie might not look as cute as the local cat does not justify its villainous reputation. Officially classified as vermin, large numbers are shot each year. For example, between 1982 and 1984 in County Cork, the Federation of Cork County Gun Clubs reported that 12,905 were shot, yet the population remains strong. They are entrepreneurs of the bird world, exploiting a niche, one step ahead of the posse! One version of a traditional rhyme concerning seeing magpies goes like this: 'One for sorrow, two for joy; three for a girl, four for a boy; five for silver, six for gold; seven for a secret, never to be told; eight for a wish, nine for a kiss; ten for a bird that's best to miss.'

Jackdaw *Corvus monedula*

Cág

Length = 33cm
Wingspan = 69–70cm
All-Ireland population: 2.8 million individuals

Rank
16
Garden
Bird Survey

Seen in
70%
of gardens
in Ireland

Identification features

A very neat-looking crow. Silver-grey nape and side of neck; rest of the head black; body a duller silver-grey; wings and tail black; pale blue eyes; beak fairly short, black and straight; legs black. **In flight:** short primary 'fingers'; flocks glide, twist and turn; often seen with rooks.

Voice guide: Voice higher pitched than rook. Includes harsh *keyaak* and *kewkaw*, sometimes repeated several times.

Diet: mainly insects, but also seeds, fruit, kitchen scraps, and any suitable food it comes across.

Food to put out: bread, seed cake, even peanuts.

Nesting Season: mid-March to mid-April.

Nest location: Found in a variety of habitats with suitable nest holes. Will use natural sites such as hollows in trees, but also regularly nests in chimneys. Nests in colonies if at all possible.

Nest: consists of sticks and twigs lined with hair, wool or fine plant material. In chimneys sticks are wedged across the flue and more twigs are built up around these, often resulting in large quantities of twigs falling down the chimney. Nest built by both the female and male. The same nest is often used year after year.

Eggs: four to six, 35mm, shiny pale blue-green eggs with usually just a light covering of grey or black flecks and spots.

Incubation period: 18–20 days by the female, fed by the male.

Fledging time: 30–33 days, young fed by both parents. May not be able to fly properly for up to a week after fledging during which time the young are dependent on the parents for food.

Number of broods reared per year: one.

Nest box: large hole-entrance box.

Average lifespan: five years.

Oldest known individual: 17 years.

Juv.

Ad.

Ad.

ℹ General information

More common in towns and cities than other crows, though numerous everywhere, except parts of the extreme west. Perhaps best known for its habit of nesting in chimney pots and is often to be seen sitting in pairs on roofs in winter. During the winter the jackdaw will move away from exposed areas such as uplands. This bird is closely associated with humans, and because of its agility it is numerous around refuse tips and scavenges on rubbish in towns and cities. Also feeds in mixed pastureland in the company of its near relative the rook. It frequently roosts in large numbers, usually at traditional woodland sites, in company with other crow species. BirdWatch Ireland's Countryside Bird Survey indicates a slight increase in population in recent years.

Confusion species

Rook (p. 160), especially young birds. No silvery grey plumage on the head, larger beak and a dark iris.

Rook *Corvus frugilegus*

Crow Rúcach/Préachán

Length = 42-47cm
Wingspan = 89–90cm
All-Ireland population: 3.75 million individuals

Rank
19
Garden
Bird Survey

Seen in
64%
of gardens
in Ireland

Identification features

All feathers are black with a purple-blue sheen; duller, sometimes dark brown when worn. Long beak looks slightly down-curved. **Adult:** outer half of beak dark; inner half and bare throat patch powdery white; black legs and untidy feathers around the thighs, giving it a 'shaggy trousers' appearance. Not as neat looking as the jackdaw. Moves slowly and deliberately on the ground, often 'galloping' away if approached. **Immature:** Rooks in their first year have an all-black beak with black feathers covering the inner half of the upper mandible. **In flight:** the primaries can clearly be seen as 'fingers' at the end of the wings, not so noticeable on jackdaws.

Voice guide: Call is a typical *kaw*, uttered on its own or repeated several times; when calling while perched or on the ground often fans its tail and stretches forward.

Diet: very varied: mainly beetles, earthworms, carrion and grain.

Food to put out: bread, tinned cat or dog food, kitchen scraps on the ground.

Nesting season: late March to the beginning of May.

Nest Location: Nests in noisy colonies in tall trees. Breeds in a variety of habitats where tall trees are present, especially near farmland.

Nest: made of sticks and twigs with some earth and lined with a variety of plant materials, and sometimes wool and hair. The same nest may be used every year following repairs. The male usually brings the nest material and the female does the building.

Eggs: three to five, 40mm, shiny, highly variable blue-green eggs covered with flecks, blotches and scribbles of grey-brown. Eggs in the same nest can vary a lot in colour and pattern.

Incubation period: 15–18 days by the female, fed by the male.

Fledging time: 31–35 days, fed by the male initially and then by both parents. The young usually stay at the colony for a few days after fledging.

Number of broods reared per year: one.

Nest box: no.

Average lifespan: five years.

Oldest known individual: 23 years.

Rookery

Ad.

Juv.

Ad.

General information

One of the first comments by visiting birdwatchers from abroad concerns the abundance of crows on this island. The rook is by far the most common crow species we have, absent only from treeless areas in the extreme west. Unlike the jackdaw, it prefers rural areas, especially where there is a good mixture of pasture and arable crops. It nests in colonies called rookeries, liking Scots pines, but any tall trees will do. Rookeries can vary from a few scattered pairs, to many hundreds of nests tightly packed together. The sound of a rookery in spring and summer is as much part of the countryside as cows and sheep. In late summer and autumn on their flight paths a large procession of crows can be seen going to roost for the night. In winter it follows very specific flight paths to roost sites that may contain thousands of individuals. BirdWatch Ireland's Countryside Bird Survey indicates a slight decrease in population in recent years.

Confusion species

Raven (not illustrated) is much bigger; massive black beak; wedge-shaped tail; very rare in gardens. Jackdaw (p. 158) is smaller; silver-grey on head; pale eyes.

Hooded Crow *Corvus cornix*

Grey or Scald Crow
Feannóg

J F M A M J J A S O N D

Length = 47cm
Wingspan = 97–98cm
All-Ireland population: 538,000 individuals

Rank
20
Garden
Bird Survey

Seen in
53%
of gardens
in Ireland

Identification features

The same size as a rook. Black hood covering head, neck and breast forms a rough-edged bib; rest of the body pale grey-brown; wings and tail black; beak long and black, legs dark. **In flight:** obvious, pale, grey-brown back. When moulting, wings can sometimes look striped black and white.

Voice guide: Its call is usually a loud hoarse *krraaa-krraaa-krraaa*.

Diet: a wide taste in food, including insects, carrion, shellfish, amphibians, eggs, nestlings and grain.

Food to put out: bread and kitchen scraps, cat or dog food on the ground.

Nesting season: late March to early May.

Nest location: Nests alone in a variety of habitats usually where tall trees are available but will also use low bushes and ledges.

Nest: a large cup-shaped nest usually built in the fork of a tree, made from sticks, twigs, moss and earth and seaweed near the coast. Lined with wool, hair and feathers.

Eggs: three to six, 43 mm, shiny eggs of various shades of pale blue-green covered with varying amounts of blotches, flecks and streaks of olive, brown, grey or black.

Incubation period: 18–20 days, by the female.

Fledging time: 28–32 days, fed by both parents.

Number of broods reared per year: one.

Nest box: no.

Average lifespan: no data available.

Oldest known individual: no data available.

Confusion species
None.

Ad.

Ad.

Juv.

ⓘ General information

This is the most widespread member of the crow family, though not as abundant as the rook. Its catholic taste in food might partly explain why it is so widespread. It is the only crow that regularly gathers food on the seashore, where it can often be seen flying up from the shore and dropping shellfish onto rocks or a nearby road to break them open. This often results in large numbers of broken shells left mysteriously on top of walls and on coastal roads. In Britain, the hooded crow is confined to Scotland and the Isle of Man, and is replaced elsewhere by the carrion crow, which has the same structure and calls but has all-black plumage. The carrion crow occurs in small numbers on our east coast and can inter-breed with the hooded crow. BirdWatch Ireland's Countryside Bird Survey indicates a slight increase in population in recent years.

Starling *Sturnus vulgaris*

Druid

Length = 21cm
Wingspan = 39–40cm
All-Ireland population: 2.7 million individuals

Rank
13
Garden Bird Survey

Seen in
77%
of gardens in Ireland

Identification features

Slightly smaller than a blackbird. **Adult in winter:** dark, glossy plumage; heavily spotted white, mostly concentrated on the head which can look pale at a distance. These spots become less obvious as spring approaches. Beak dark, pointed, legs dull pink. **Adult in summer:** black plumage with blue and green sheen; few spots, restricted to back and towards tail; beak straw yellow, very pale blue-grey base on males; legs pink. **Immature:** dusty grey-brown; pale throat, pale buff edges to wing feathers; beak black; legs dark brown-red. Rarely seen singly; always quarrelling and noisy. **In flight:** all dark; pointed triangular shaped wings; short, fanned tail.

Voice guide: The calls and songs of the starling are very varied and it is an expert mimic, not only of other birds but also of artificial sounds like a referee's whistle, doorbells and even car alarms, all mixed up together.

Diet: varied but mainly insects, berries and seeds; usually feeds on ground.

Food to put out: bread, seed cake and peanuts.

Nesting season: early April to end May.

Nest location: Will nest in a variety of rural and urban habitats, in cavities in trees and roofs or eaves.

Nest: a rough collection of twigs and other plant materials, also man-made materials such as plastic, etc., with a cup lined with feathers. Usually started by the male and finished by the female.

Eggs: four to six, 30mm, slightly shiny pale blue or white eggs. Incubation period: 12–15 days, by both parents.

Fledging time: 19–22 days, fed by both parents. Young dependent on parents for a while after leaving the nest, often seen chasing them and begging for food.

Number of broods reared per year: one to two.

Nest box: hole-entrance box.

Average lifespan: five years.

Oldest known individual: 17 years.

Ad. Br.

Juv. moulting
to 1st W.

Ad. W.

Juv.

General information

Common and widespread, absent only from some upland areas. The starling catches insects by sticking its long, thin beak into grass and opening it wide, causing any insects to fall into the space, which can then be easily caught if suitable. In the late autumn and winter, starlings form large flocks, often landing on pylons and overhead wires, before wheeling around in pre-roost flights. The roost is typically in woods and reed beds or on cliffs or buildings. These flocks often contain many thousands of birds, sometimes as many as 100,000. Each winter, Irish starlings are joined by birds from Britain, Scandinavia, Germany, Poland and Russia. In severe continental winters, many more come and as many as 6 to 8 million may spend the winter here. BirdWatch Ireland's Countryside Bird Survey indicates a slight decrease in population in recent years.

Confusion species

Blackbird (p. 124) is bigger, no spots, long tail, dark legs.

House Sparrow *Passer domesticus*

Gealbhan binne

Length = 15cm
Wingspan = 23–24cm
All-Ireland population: 2.4 million individuals

Rank
9
Garden
Bird Survey

Seen in
82%
of gardens
in Ireland

Identification features

Slightly larger than a robin. **Male:** black bib, smaller in the winter; grey crown; dark brown eye-stripe extends and widens back and down the nape. Ear coverts and side of throat pale grey, sometimes looking almost white. Breast and belly pencil-grey; tail relatively long, dark-brown with paler buff edges to the feathers; rump grey; back streaked light and dark brown; wings light and dark brown; white wing bar. Short, stout, conical dark-grey beak, pink legs. **Female:** no distinctive plumage features, paler than the male, lacking the black, white and richer browns, brown above, paler below. **In flight:** fast and straight, undulates on longer flights.

Voice guide: The call is a loud *cheep*, repeated without variation. Often heard calling and chattering in groups from bushes or hedges, where their dull plumage makes them almost invisible, despite the loud, repetitive noise.

Diet: seeds, berries; nestlings fed mainly insects.

Food to put out: seed cake, seed, peanuts, kitchen scraps and bread.

Nesting season: late March to mid-July.

Nest location: Usually nests in holes and cavities in buildings and walls, especially near farmland. Will sometimes build in dense vegetation.

Nest: If not in a cavity, nest will usually have a dome of some description on it. Made of a variety of plant materials and also man-made materials such as string, cloth, plastic. The cup is usually lined with feathers or hair. Built mainly by the male.

Eggs: three to five, 22mm, slightly shiny cream or pale blue eggs covered with spots, flecks and blotches ranging in colour from dark brown to green-grey, yellow-grey or black.

Incubation period: 13–15 days, mainly by the female.

Fledging time: 15–17 days, fed by both parents.

Number of broods reared per year: two to three.

Nest box: hole-entrance box.

Average lifespan: three years.

Oldest known individual: 12 years.

F.

F.

Br. M.

M. NBr.

ⓘ General information

With an estimated world population of 500 million, the house sparrow is considered to be one of the most widespread and numerous land-bird species in the world. It is encountered everywhere and is most numerous in the eastern half of the island. As the name suggests it has been associated with man for a long time. Can often be seen 'dust-bathing' in dust or sand, usually in small groups. This is thought to help remove parasites and keep plumage in good condition. It is a sedentary species and has declined in some areas in recent years. Changes in farming practices, crop spraying and the use of pesticides in gardens are contributing factors. The decline has been far more dramatic in Britain. One study showed that cats accounted for 30 per cent of house sparrow deaths in one village in England. BirdWatch Ireland's Countryside Bird Survey indicates a slight increase in population in recent years.

Confusion species

Tree sparrow (p. 168) is very local and scarce; differs in head pattern with crown completely chestnut-brown; cheeks white with isolated black spot; sexes similar. Female house sparrows may resemble female chaffinches (p. 170) but lack obvious white wing bars.

Tree Sparrow *Passer montanus*

Gealbhan crainn

Length = 13–14cm
Wingspan = 21cm
All-Ireland population: 9,000 breeding pairs

Rank
40
Garden Bird Survey

Seen in
6%
of gardens in Ireland

Identification features

Same size as house sparrow. Unlike the house sparrow, male and female tree sparrows are identical in appearance. The body colours are similar to that of the house sparrow: back, wings and tail a complex mixture of light and dark browns and white, but the head pattern is completely different. The crown and nape are bright red-brown; the ear coverts are white with a black spot; the lores (the area between the eye and beak) are black; and they have a noticeable, incomplete white collar. **In flight:** like the house sparrow, fast and straight over short distances, undulates on longer flights.

Voice guide: Similar calls to house sparrow, however the note is shriller, *teck teck* or *chip chip*.

Diet: mainly small seeds; chicks are usually fed insects.

Food to put out: peanuts and seed mix.

Nesting season: mid-April to June.

Nest location: usually anywhere there is a cavity in trees, walls, behind climbers such as ivy or in the eves of buildings.

Nest: cup-shaped but may also have a dome, not very neat, made from twigs and dead plant material and lined with feathers. Nest built by both the female and male.

Eggs: three to six, 20mm, shiny white or buff ground colour with heavy dark brown blotches, speckles and streaks, occasionally paler.

Incubation period: 12–14 days, by the female and male.

Fledging time: 12–14 days, fed by male at first, while female broods the chicks, then by both parents.

Number of broods reared per year: two to three.

Nest box: will use a blue-tit-type box.

Average lifespan: two to three years.

Oldest known individual: 11 years.

General information

Unlike its much more common relative, the tree sparrow is only regularly found not too far from the coast in the north and east. Its name suggests it likes trees, but it is not usually seen in woods and forests. Its preferred agricultural habitat in Ireland – cereal farmland with thick hedgerows containing small bushes and trees – is subject to major change and may be a factor in its scarcity. In winter it will often be found in mixed flocks of seed-eating birds in stubbles and even on landfill sites.

Confusion species

House sparrow (p. 166) is duller-looking overall, lacking the chestnut cap and black cheek spot.

Chaffinch *Fringilla coelebs*

Rí rua

J F M A M J J A S O N D

Length = 15–16cm
Wingspan = 25–26cm
All-Ireland population: 4.21 million individuals

Rank
5
Garden
Bird Survey

Seen in
95%
of gardens
in Ireland

Identification features

Slightly larger than a robin. **Male:** face, breast and belly rosy orange-pink; undertail white; crown and nape metallic blue-grey; back brown; rump olive-green. Wings dark brown with two white wing bars; white outer tail feathers on a relatively long dark tail. Males in their first year and during the winter are duller, though not as dull as the females. Stout, conical, grey beak; pale-pink legs. **Female:** same pattern as male but body drab pale grey-brown. Beak paler. **In flight:** double white wing bar and white outer tail feathers very obvious. White underwing.

Voice guide: Calls include a loud *buzz-twink-twink-twink* and in flight a low, weak weiou. Its song, which lasts about three seconds and is repeated, starts with buzzing notes, slows and descends into a jumble and finally a flourish.

Diet: mainly insects during the summer and in the winter a wide variety of seeds, berries, etc.; broadest diet of all finches.

Food to put out: seed and seedcake, usually on the ground; also peanuts. The chaffinch can often be seen on the ground under a bird table or feeder, eating seeds and bits of peanuts dropped by other birds.

Nesting season: mid-April to end May.

Nest location: in a variety of habitats with trees, from woodlands to hedgerows and gardens; usually built in the fork of a tree.

Nest: a cup-shaped nest, made from a variety of plant materials and spiders' webs, lined with feathers and fine plant material.

Eggs: four to five, 19mm, shiny eggs ranging from white to pale pink or brown with a scattering of dark red-brown spots and streaks.

Incubation period: 11–13 days, by the female.

Fledging time: 12–16 days fed by both parents.

Number of broods reared per year: one.

Nest box: no.

Average lifespan: three years.

Oldest known individual: 12 years.

F.

F.

NBr. M.

Br. M.

ℹ️ General information

Chaffinches are one of the most abundant and widespread breeding bird species in Ireland. They nest in woodlands, hedgerows and gardens. Irish chaffinches are sedentary, with most breeding pairs returning to the same nest site year after year. In the winter, large numbers of chaffinches arrive here from northern Europe, via European countries bordering the south shore of the North Sea. Outside the breeding season, chaffinches mainly eat seeds, and over a hundred different seed types have been recorded being eaten by them, which is one possible explanation for their abundance in Ireland. BirdWatch Ireland's Countryside Bird Survey indicates a slight decrease in population in recent years.

Confusion species

Brambling (p. 172) is an uncommon winter visitor; white rump; male more orange than red; less white on wings. Greenfinch (p. 174): absence of white on females and immatures. Female house sparrow (p. 166) has no white on outer tail feathers and no obvious white on the wings.

Brambling *Fringilla montifringilla*

Breacán

J F M A M J J A S O N D

Length = 14cm
Wingspan = 25–26cm
Winter population: no data

Rank
34
Garden
Bird Survey

Seen in
10%
of gardens
in Ireland

Identification features

Same size as a robin. **Upperparts:** Male has black and grey hood becoming all black in summer, closely flecked light and dark brown mantle, pale wing bar, noticeable oblong white rump patch, dark tail, no obvious white outer tail feathers. Female, duller and paler grey on the face. **Underparts:** orange throat and breast; white belly, cream flanks with some dark spots, white undertail coverts. Female duller. Beak short, conical, yellow with a dark tip. Legs dark brown. **In flight:** undulating, complex upperparts pattern and white rump clearly visible.

Voice guide: The call is a quick loud sharp *scheep-scheep*.

Diet: seeds, especially beechmast and berries.
Food to put out: seed on the ground, occasionally seed cake and peanuts.
Nesting season: Does not breed in Ireland. Breeds in Scandinavia and Russia from mid-May to July in woodland.
Nest: like that of the chaffinch, a cup-shaped nest, usually built in the fork of a tree. Made from a variety of plant materials and spiders' webs, lined with feathers and fine plant material. Built by the female.
Eggs: five to seven, 19mm, shiny light-blue eggs with large pale blotches of red or pink and a few spots of dark red-brown.
Incubation period: 11–13 days, by the female.
Fledging time: 11–13 days, fed by both parents.
Number of broods reared per year: one.
Nest box: no.
Average lifespan: no data available.
Oldest known individual: eight years.

NBr. M.

NBr. F.

NBr. F.

NBr. M.

General information

The brambling is an uncommon winter visitor to Ireland, more abundant in some years than others. Flocks of over 300 have occasionally been seen. Particularly attracted to beechmast. Usually seen with chaffinches. Can turn up any time from October to March or early April in variable but small numbers, a rare visitor to gardens.

Confusion species

Chaffinch (p. 170) has no white rump patch and lacks orange plumage.

Greenfinch *Carduelis chloris*

Glasán darach

Length = 15cm
Wingspan = 25–26cm
All-Ireland population: 830,000 individuals

Rank
10
Garden Bird Survey

Seen in
81%
of gardens in Ireland

Identification features

Slightly larger than a robin. **Male:** bright yellow-green; bright yellow patches on the wings and base of the outer tail feathers; grey on wings and ear coverts; strong conical beak often pink at the base; pink legs. **Female:** drab, paler yellow patches. Male and female both have a dark shadow around the eye. **Immature:** indistinctly streaked below and may resemble female chaffinch. **In flight:** undulating flight; flashes yellow and green.

Voice guide: Calls include a squeaky *whou-ie-ouh*, and buzzing notes. Will sometimes sing during a display flight, with stiff mechanical wing beats. Parts of its long, melodious, twittering song are often likened to that of a canary.

Diet: mainly seeds; nestlings are fed insects and seeds.

Food to put out: peanuts, seed and seed cake.

Nesting season: early April to late June.

Nest location: Nests in a variety of open woodland habits, hedgerows and gardens. Usually built in trees or bushes, close to the trunk.

Nest: a substantial cup-shaped nest made of a variety of plant materials lined with strands of plant material, hair and sometimes feathers.

Eggs: four to six, 20mm, shiny cream or pale blue-green eggs with a scattering of spots and blotches ranging in colour from red-brown to black.

Incubation period: 13–15 days, by the female.

Fledging time: 14–16 days. Fed by both parents who, unlike many garden birds, regurgitate food for their young.

Number of broods reared per year: two to three.

Nest box: open-front box.

Average lifespan: two years.

Oldest known individual: 12 years.

F.

Br. M.

Juv.

NBr. M.

ℹ️ General information

The greenfinch frequents arable farmland and suburban areas, so it is not too surprising that it is more common in the east and south. The increased use of herbicides on farmland has contributed to its decline in recent years. In winter only a few additional birds come to Ireland, mainly from Britain. As winter progresses and the supply of seed diminishes, greenfinches form large flocks, some-times containing over a hundred birds. They are regular visitors to bird tables and fight fiercely between themselves and with other species for the best place on the peanut feeder. Threatening with its beak open and wings spread, two greenfinches will often tangle upwards into the air with a flurry of wings before separating. Bird-Watch Ireland's Countryside Bird Survey indicates a decrease in population in recent years.

Confusion species

Siskin (p. 178) is smaller. Male Siskin: black cap and chin; female and immature: very streaked; black and yellow wings. Female chaffinch (p. 170) has white wing bars and no bright yellow feathers.

Goldfinch *Carduelis carduelis*

Lasair choille

Length = 14cm
Wingspan = 23–24cm
All-Ireland population: 916,000 individuals

Rank
8
Garden Bird Survey

Seen in
85%
of gardens in Ireland

Identification features

Same size as a robin. **Upperparts:** Blood-red face; broad bright yellow wing bars; rest of wings black, with white tips to the primaries and secondaries; tail black and white; back is pale golden brown; rump is paler again. Stout, pink conical beak with a dark tip; pink legs. **Underside:** white with broad golden-brown flanks; incomplete sandy-brown breast band. Birds just out of the nest are similar to the adults except that the head is completely pale brown. **In flight:** striking yellow and black wing pattern and undulating flight.

Voice guide: It has a long beautiful song, containing buzzes, characteristic fluid notes, trills and twitters. Calls almost continuously in flight. The call is simpler than the song and contains more fluid notes.

Diet: a variety of seeds, especially teasels and thistles; some insects in summer.

Food to put out: peanuts, sunflower and Nyjer seed.

Nesting season: late April to mid-July.

Nest location: Nests in a wide variety of habitats with trees including gardens. Nest usually built towards the end of branches, not in dense cover. Like many of its relatives, it nests in loose colonies.

Nest: a tidy cup-shaped nest made of a variety of plant materials and lined with light plant material, wool, hair and/or feathers. Built by the female.

Eggs: four to six, 18mm, shiny cream or pale blue-green eggs with a scattering of small spots and blotches ranging in colour from red-brown to black, mainly at the broad end of the egg.

Incubation period: 13–15 days, by female who is fed by male.

Fledging time: 13–16 days, fed by both parents. Young remain dependent on the parents for about a week after leaving the nest.

Number of broods reared per year: two to three.

Nest box: no.

Average lifespan: two years.

Oldest known individual: eight years.

Confusion species

None.

Juv.

Ad.

General information

Goldfinches declined in numbers in the 19th century due to large-scale trapping, especially in the northern half of the island. The introduction of laws protecting birds in the 20th century has reduced this activity, but illegal trapping still continues in some parts. In Ireland the goldfinch is sedentary by nature. It is not easy to see as it is constantly on the move, searching for its main food – thistles and teasels. It is the only finch that can extract the seeds from the teasel (a plant used widely for flower-arranging). It will also feed on the seeds of knapweed, ragwort, groundsel and dandelions. In the last 20 years goldfinches have become increasingly common visitors to gardens, visiting peanut and seed feeders. BirdWatch Ireland's Countryside Bird Survey indicates an increase in population in recent years.

Siskin *Carduelis spinus*

Píobaire

J F M A M J J A S O N D

Length = 12cm
Wingspan = 21–22cm
All-Ireland population: 60,000
breeding pairs

Rank
18
Garden
Bird Survey

Seen in
64%
of gardens
in Ireland

Identification features

Same size as a blue tit. **Male:** black cap and throat; head dark olive green with pale yellow stripe extending from the eye back to the nape and down around the ear coverts; wings black with two bright yellow wing bars and pale edges to the secondaries; back olive green with faint dark streaks; rump yellow, short notched tail with yellow patches at base of outer feathers; breast and upper belly green-yellow; lower belly and undertail coverts white with dark streaking. Short, pale, conical beak, and dark grey legs. **Female:** no black cap or chin; not as yellow, especially on the wings; heavier streaking on the back. **Immature:** paler and more streaked than female. **In flight:** small, yellow and black; fast and undulating.

Voice guide: Calls and song include a variable twitter, a very thin *tee-oou,* a buzzing *wheeeze* and a high, bouncing, chattering trill.

Diet: seeds, especially conifer seeds, alder and birch. Siskins will also take insects from the undersides of leaves in summer and autumn.

Food to put out: peanuts and Nyjer seed.

Nesting season: early April to end May.

Nest location: Nests mainly in coniferous or mixed woodlands. Usually built towards the end of a branch, may be high up.

Nest: a cup-shaped nest made of small twigs, lichens and mosses and other plant material. Lined with strands of plant material, hair, wool and feathers.

Eggs: three to five, 16 mm, shiny pale blue eggs with a light scattering of red-brown and purple blotches and streaks.

Incubation period: 12–14 days, by the female.

Fledging time: 13–15 days. Fed initially by the male, while the female broods the young, then by both parents, delivering food by regurgitation.

Number of broods reared per year: two.

Nest Box: no.

Average lifespan: no data available.

Oldest known individual: nine years.

F.

F.

M.

M.

F.

ℹ️ General information

Breeds mainly in coniferous plantations, particularly spruce. The recent increase in forestry plantations has led to a corresponding increase in its population. In winter it is has become a regular visitor to bird tables where it can be very aggressive despite its small size. It has a characteristic habit of perching upside down when feeding from peanut feeders. It is said that siskins are particularly attracted to peanut feeders with red mesh. Numbers visiting gardens vary from year to year, depending on the availability of natural food supplies, such as birch and alder seeds, usually turning up in gardens from December onwards. Often associates with redpolls.

Confusion species

Greenfinch (p. 174) is much bigger, obvious large conical beak, no streaking on the plumage. Redpoll (p. 182) lacks yellow plumage and males have a red forehead and black chin.

Linnet *Carduelis cannabina*

Gleoiseach

Length = 14cm
Wingspan = 23–24cm
All-Ireland population: 556,000 individuals

Rank
32
Garden
Bird Survey

Seen in
11%
of gardens
in Ireland

Identification features

Same size as a robin. **Male:** bright red forehead and breast patches in summer; rest of the head grey; white belly; back rich brown; wings darker brown; bright white edges to the primaries; tail notched and edged white. Duller in the winter, lacking the red plumage. Short, conical dark-grey beak; dark-grey legs. **Female and immature:** browner, streaked, no red or grey. **In flight:** bouncing flight, diffuse white flashes on wings, calls constantly.

Voice guide: Its flight call is squeaky, like a wet cork rubbed against glass. Its song is often a very long series of chirps, twitters, chatters and musical, warbling notes. Often sings from the top of a bush or tree.

Diet: a wide variety of seeds, especially thistles.
Food to put out: seed on the ground.
Nesting season: mid-April to early July.
Nest location: Found in areas of low bushes such as gorse patches; also in hedgerow and occasionally gardens with suitable bushes. A number of pairs may be found nesting in a small area.
Nest: a bulky cup made of grass and other plant materials, lined with hair, wool and sometimes feathers.
Eggs: four to five, 18mm, slightly shiny pale blue or blue-green eggs with a light scattering of red or purple brown spots or blotches. Eggs may sometimes be unmarked.
Incubation period: 11–14 days, by the female.
Fledging time: 12–14 days. Fed by male at first while female broods the chicks, then by both parents.
Number of broods reared per year: two to three.
Nest box: no.
Average lifespan: two years.
Oldest known individual: eight years.

. M.

F.

F./1st W.

Br. M.

NBr. M.

General information

This finch is associated with cultivated land though can be found anywhere where weed seeds are available, from high ground to seashore and islands. It is surprisingly scarce in south-west Ulster. During the winter, many of our linnets migrate to France and Spain, and those that remain rarely travel far, but form flocks of up to 200 birds or more. The linnet usually mixes with other finch species and when disturbed will fly around in a circle before returning to the ground. Sadly, like many wild birds associated with farming, the linnet has declined noticeably in the last 20 years and intensification of farming, with the associated increase in the use of herbicides and hedge-removal, may be the cause.

Confusion species

Redpoll (see p. 182) is smaller. Small, pale beak; black chin; pale wing bar and heavier streaking on the body.

Redpoll *Carduelis flammea*

Deargéadan/Gleoisín cúldearg

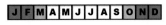

Length = 12–13cm
Wingspan = 21–22cm
All-Ireland population: 298,000 individuals

Rank
25
Garden Bird Survey

Seen in
42%
of gardens in Ireland

Identification features

Slightly larger than a blue tit. **Male:** blood-red forehead; black bib; back streaked light and dark brown; wings darker with two pale buff wing bars, the inner one being very faint; rump pale with faint dark streaks; tail short and slightly notched; breast deep pink in breeding season, buff in winter; belly and undertail coverts white; flanks heavily streaked light and dark brown; short, stubby, pale yellow beak; legs short and black. **Female and immature:** no red, duller and more streaked. **In flight:** very bouncy flight.

Voice guide: Calls and song include a high, thin rising *oiu-eeee*, also short, fast reeling notes and a *chi-chi-chi-chaa*.

Diet: mainly seeds; birch and alder seeds form the main part of diet. Will eat insects during the summer.

Food to put out: peanuts and Nyjer seed.

Nesting season: early May to mid-July.

Nest location: Nests in birch and conifer woodlands/plantations and open scrub areas. The nest is built in a tree or bush anywhere from very close to the ground to high in a tree. Will sometime nest close to other nesting redpolls.

Nest: an untidy cup made of small twigs, grass and other plant material, lined with strands of fine plant material, hair and/or feathers.

Eggs: four to five, 17mm, slightly shiny pale green-blue eggs with a light scattering of red-brown flecks and blotches, most towards the broad end of the egg.

Incubation period: 11–14 days, by the female while being fed by the male.

Fledging time: 14–16 days. Fed by male at first while female broods the chicks, then by both parents.

Number of broods reared per year: two.

Nest box: no.

Average lifespan: unknown.

Oldest known individual: eight years.

M.

M.

F./1st W.

 ### General information

A bird typical of coniferous and mixed woodlands, the redpoll breeds mainly in the north-western half of the country. It has declined as a breeding species in recent years, especially in the south-eastern half of the country. In winter it is rarely found far from alders and birch, feeding acrobatically, often in the company of siskins. Redpolls of the north European and Greenland races, which are paler, have been seen in Ireland. BirdWatch Ireland's Countryside Bird Survey indicates an increase in population in recent years.

Confusion species

Linnet (p. 180) is bigger; grey beak; less streaked; white on the wings. Siskin (p. 178) is similar in size and body pattern but has yellow patches and no red on the head.

Bullfinch *Pyrrhula pyrrhula*

Corcrán coille

Length = 16cm
Wingspan = 25–26cm
All-Ireland population: 496,000
individuals

Rank
24
Garden
Bird Survey

Seen in
43%
of gardens
in Ireland

Identification features

A large fat finch, larger than a robin, plump in proportion. **Male:** jet-black crown and nape; throat, breast and belly vivid, deep pink; light grey back; black wings with a broad white wing bar; large white rump patch (best seen in flight); black tail; undertail coverts white; short, stout, dark, conical beak; dark grey legs. **Female:** vivid pink replaced by dull pale grey-brown; back also grey-brown. **Immature:** like female but lacks black cap. **In flight:** bouncing flight, always showing bright white rump.

Voice guide: Song is a soft whistling chatter, the call a weak, soft *weeep*.

Diet: berries and other fruit, and emerging buds. Will feed insects to nestlings.

Food to put out: Will occasionally take seed on the ground.

Nesting season: late April to mid-July.

Nest location: usually in a bush about 1–2m off the ground in areas with trees and low bushes and undergrowth, hedgerows and gardens.

Nest: a cup-shaped nest of small twigs, moss and lichens, usually lined with strands of plant material and hair. Built by the female.

Eggs: four to five, 20 mm, shiny pale green-blue eggs with dark brown or black spots and blotches mainly near the broad end of the egg.

Incubation period: 13–15 days, by the female while being fed by the male.

Fledging time: 14–16 days. Fed by male at first while female broods the chicks, then by both parents.

Number of broods reared per year: two to three.

Nest box: no.

Average lifespan: two years.

Oldest known individual: nine years.

F.

Juv.

M.

M.

F.

ℹ️ General information

This finch is widespread in Ireland, being absent only from the extreme west and at high altitudes. Despite the colourful plumage of the male, it is not seen very often, though the soft contact call is a feature of our mixed native hedgerows. In fact, seeing an emerging bird with the large white rump patch is often the first indication of its presence. Between February and April if seed supplies are low it will take to eating buds from fruit trees (research has shown that a fruit tree can lose up to 50 per cent of its buds in spring without affecting the crop). Bullfinches are a sedentary species, usually seen alone or in pairs. Recent farming trends such as intensification of farming and hedgerow removal have contributed to their decline in some areas. Despite this BirdWatch Ireland's Countryside Bird Survey indicates an increase in population in recent years.

Confusion species

Male chaffinch (p. 170) lacks black on the head and breast not as red.

Yellowhammer *Emberiza citronella*

Buíóg

Length = 16–17cm
Wingspan = 25–26cm
All-Ireland population: 230,000 individuals

Rank
39
Garden Bird Survey

Seen in
6%
of gardens in Ireland

Identification features

Summer: male has bright yellow head, female duller; back, wings and tail a complex mixture of light and dark browns; rump bright red-brown; yellow throat and breast, streaked on female; chestnut side of breast and streaked flanks on male. **Winter:** dull-looking; males and females similar in appearance, heavy grey-brown streaking on head, throat, breast and flanks, with yellow tinges to the head, throat and lower belly. **In flight:** undulating flight, looks long and slim. White outer tail feathers; rusty coloured rump.

Voice guide: In spring and summer the yellowhammer is often first located by its distinctive song delivered from a prominent hedgerow bush or tree. It is a loud clear wheezing song, with the notes spaced as if saying rather quickly *'little-bit-of-bread-and-no-cheeeeese'*. At other times of the year its call is a short rough *schep*.

Diet: mainly seeds of large grasses and cereals.

Food to put out: Will take seed on the ground.

Nesting season: May to July.

Nest location: Usually found in tillage farmland and sometimes woodland. It normally nests on the ground in tall grasses near hedges, walls or bushes.

Nest: cup-shaped, made of grass and dead plant material, usually lined with hair and fine plant strands. Usually built by the female.

Eggs: three to five, 20–21mm, slightly shiny white, grey or pale blue eggs with dark blotches, streaks and fine flecks.

Incubation period: 12–14 days, usually by the female.

Fledging time: 14–16 days, fed by male at first while female broods the chicks, then by both parents. Will leave the nest before being able to fly.

Number of broods reared per year: two.

Nest box: no.

Average lifespan: two to three years.

Oldest known individual: 11 years.

Br. M.

F.

Ad. Br. M.

NBr. M.

 General information

The male sings with head held high from a wall, the top of a bush, or a post in open farmland. In winter yellowhammers sometimes form flocks containing up to a hundred birds. Does not travel far from its place of birth and is most numerous in the east and south, and across the midlands, reflecting the distribution of cereal farming in Ireland. It has declined dramatically in the last 20 years, particularly in the west and north. Areas where tillage comprises less than ten per cent of land-use have seen large declines. Also, the switch from spring to autumn sowing of cereals has meant a reduction in stubbles and fewer food sources in winter.

Confusion species

Reed bunting (p. 188); females and immatures may look superficially similar; lacks yellow plumage; darker head, white moustachial stripe; grey-brown rump.

Reed Bunting *Emberiza schoeniclus*

Gealóg ghiolcaí

Length = 15–16cm
Wingspan = 24cm
All-Ireland population: 217,000 individuals

Rank
44
Garden
Bird Survey

Seen in
4%
of gardens
in Ireland

Identification features

About the same size as a robin. **Male:** very striking in summer plumage. Black head, white neck collar and moustache; back heavily streaked dark brown and buff; rump grey; wings have rich brown tones, no white; tail long and black with white outer feathers; underside pale grey; black streaks on the flanks. **Female and immature:** less striking; dark brown heads, white throat and moustache; faint white supercilium; no white neck collar. In winter males resemble females, and the plumage is paler. **In flight:** undulating; rarely flies far; chestnut on wings; white outer tail feathers.

Voice guide: Call is a high, thin, descending *tzeeeu*. Its song, usually sung from a prominent position, is a high, hesitant, buzzing variation on *weeet-weet-chit* and a lower, faster *chi-choo*.

Diet: During the breeding season feeds on insects, changing to seeds of small grasses and herbs in winter.

Food to put out: Will occasionally take seed on the ground.

Nesting season: late April to mid-July.

Nest location: Usually nests on the ground not far from water, in reed beds, bogs and along ditches, also in young conifer plantations.

Nest: a cup-shaped nest of grass, moss and lichens, usually lined with fine strands of plant material and hair. Built by the female.

Eggs: four to six, 20 mm, shiny pale green-blue eggs with dark brown or black spots, lines and blotches mainly near the broad end of the egg.

Incubation period: 13–15 days, mainly by the female.

Fledging time: 11–15 days. Fed by male at first while female broods the chicks, then by both parents.

Number of broods reared per year: two to three.

Nest box: no.

Average lifespan: two years.

Oldest known individual: nine years.

NBr. M.

Br. F.

Br. M.

F.

General information

A common breeding species throughout the island often asso-ciated with wet and marginal ground. During the winter the reed bunting roams in small mixed flocks over open ground in search of food. Has declined in numbers in recent times, due mainly to modern farming practices and habitat loss.

Confusion species

Yellowhammer (p. 186); superficially females and immatures may look similar; more yellow-looking; no white moustachial stripe; rust-coloured rump.

Glossary

Band: usually used to describe a distinct line of light or dark colour on the tail of a bird. For example on a young gull or on the undertail of a collared dove.

Bars/barring: refers to distinct light or dark lines formed by light or dark feathers or feather parts such as the yellow wing bar on a greenfinch or the orange and white bars on the breast of a male sparrowhawk, see image p. 83.

Bins/binos: birdwatchers' terms for binoculars.

Birder/birding: birdwatcher/bird watching.

Bird of prey: a term used to describe any bird species that hunts and eats other birds, mammals and other higher vertebrates. Usually includes the owls. See also 'raptor'.

Breeding season: that period of the bird's year when it sets up territory, builds a nest and rears young until they are able to fly.

Brood: two meanings. Either a collective name for the chicks hatched by a pair of birds or the action of sitting on very young chicks to keep them warm.

Colony: a group of birds nesting in close proximity to each other such as house martins or black-headed gulls.

Coverts: groups of feathers that cover the base of other feathers, see illustration p. 61.

Crop: a word used to describe a sac between the mouth and stomach of a bird, used to store food to be eaten later or regurgitated to feed chicks.

Dip: to dip in birdwatching is to miss seeing a new, rare or scarce species. You dipped or dipped out by not seeing the bird.

Fall: this is when a large number of migrant birds arrive at a location at the one time. For example at Cape Clear in autumn, hundreds of meadow pipits or goldcrests will arrive on the island overnight, in suitable weather conditions. This is referred to as a 'fall' of migrants.

First-winter/second summer/second winter, etc: some species such as the gulls take two to four years to reach adult plumage. During this period they can be aged on their plumage appearance. Therefore a black-headed gull in its first winter after hatching can be specifically identified as a 'first-winter' black-headed gull'.

Fledge/fledging: refers to the time when a young bird finally leaves the nest and is able to fly.

Immature: refers to any bird that has not reached maturity, usually used for birds that have distinct plumage characteristics when immature such as gulls.

Jizz: a combination of characteristics which identify a living bird, but which may not be distinguished individually.

Leading edge: the front part of the outstretched wing from the body to the wing tip. See illustration p. 61.

On passage: refers to a bird seen during migration passing through to somewhere further north or south. See also 'passage migrant'.

Passage migrant: a bird that visits Ireland while migrating from its winter to summer areas and vice versa.

Passerine: a bird belonging to the order of Passeriformes or perching birds.

Population explosion: a phenomenon which occurs when feeding and breeding conditions suddenly improve for a species, resulting in a sudden rise in its population.

Primaries: long feathers at the tip of the wing, see illustration p. 61.

Phyllosc: a term used when a small warbler showing characteristics of the genus *Phylloscopus* is seen but cannot be specifically identified. Other warbler genera which are often abbreviated include *Hippolais* (hippo), and *Acrocephalus* (acro).

Raptor: a term used to describe hawks, falcons, eagles or buzzards, but not usually owls.

Ringing: the act of placing a very light metal ring on a bird, by a highly trained and licensed bird ringer. The birds are usually caught in very fine nets called 'mist nets' which do not harm them.

Roost: When birds sleep, sometimes used when describing places where a number of birds sleep together such as a swallow roost in a reed bed or a wren roost in thick ivy.

Rodenticides: chemicals used to kill rodents such as rats and mice.

Secondaries: a row of feathers along the trailing edge of the wing, see illustration p. 61.

Sedentary: refers to a bird that does not move far from where it hatched.

'Scope: a term used for a telescope by some birders/birdwatchers.

Summer/winter: In bird-watching these terms do not always follow the dictionary definition. For example, winter often refers to the period from October to the end of March, especially when discussing 'winter visitors' such as redwing and fieldfare. Likewise, summer can refer to the period from late March to the end of August when discussing 'summer visitors' such as swallows.

Tick: When some birders/birdwatchers see a new species they call it a 'tick' because they tick it off on their checklist of birds.

Twitcher: someone who is interested in rare or scarce birds, sometimes travelling long distances at short notice to try and see a species which they have never seen before and add it to their list.

Undergrowth: usually refers to low bushes, brambles, tall grasses and wild flowers, often packed tight together.

Upperparts: usually used when describing feathers seen on a bird when viewed from above.

Undertail: usually used when describing the appearance of the tail of a bird when viewed from below.

Vagrant: a bird species that is scarce or rare, usually blown off course on migration.

Wing span: the distance from wing tip to wing tip on a bird when the wings are fully extended.

Plumage: the feathers on a bird.

Scavenger: usually used to describe a bird, such as a magpie, that has a very broad diet, eating almost anything it comes across.

Song: this refers to the sounds made by birds during courtship and breeding, usually used to attract a mate or defend a territory.

Supercilium: feathers between the eye and the top of the head, usually used if they form a distinct line or 'eyebrow' such as on a redwing. See illustration p. 61.

Territory: the area of land defended by a bird, usually from others of the same species, which contains its nest during the breeding season.

Trailing edge: the rear part of the outstretched wing from the body to the wing tip. See illustration p. 61.

Undulating flight: bouncing up and down in flight. See illustration p. 62.

Bibliography

Armstrong E.A. *The Folklore of Birds*. Collins (London, 1958)

Balmer, D.E., Gillings, S., Caffrey, B.J., Swann, R.L., Downie, I. and Fuller, R.J. *Bird Atlas 2007–11: The Breeding and Wintering Birds of Britain and Ireland*. British Trust for Ornithology (Thetford 2013)

Buczacki, S. *Garden Natural History*. Collins (London, 2007)

Campbell B. & Lack, E. *A Dictionary of Birds*. T & AD Poyser (Carlton, 1985)

Crowe, O., Coombes, R.H., O'Sullivan, O., Tierney, T.D., Walsh, A.J. *Countryside Bird Survey Report 1998–2013* (Wicklow 2014)

Cooper Foster, J. *Ulster Folklore*. Carter (Belfast, 1951)

Dempsey, E. & O'Clery, M. *The Complete Guide to Ireland's Birds*. Gill & Macmillan (Dublin, 1993)

du Feu, C. *Nestboxes*. British Trust for Ornithology (Hertfordshire, 1985)

Gibbons, D.W., Reid, J.B., & Chapman, R. A. *The New Atlas of Breeding Birds in Britain and Ireland 1988–1991*. T. & A.D. Poyser (Carlton, 1993)

Ginn, H.B. & Melville, D.S. *Moult in Birds*. British Trust for Ornithology (Tring, 1983)

Hagemeijer, W.J.M & Blair, M.J. *The EBCC Atlas of European Breeding Birds: Their Distribution and Abundance*. T. & A.D. Poyser (1997)

Harrison, C. *A Field Guide to the Nests, Eggs and Nestlings of British and European Birds*. Collins (London, 1975)

Hutchinson, C.D. *Birds in Ireland*. T. & A.D. Poyser (Carlton, 1989)

Jonsson, L. *Birds of Europe with North Africa and the Middle East*. Christopher Helm Publishers Ltd (London, 1992)

Joyce, P.W. *Irish Names of Places, Vol. I*. Phoenix Publishing Company (Dublin, 1913)

Lack, P. *The Atlas of Wintering Birds in Britain and Ireland*. T. & A.D. Poyser (Carlton, 1986)

Lewington, R. *Guide to Garden Wildlife*. British Wildlife Publishing (Gillingham, 2008)

Mead, C. *The State of the Nation's Birds*. Whittet (Suffolk, 2000)

Moriarty, C. *A Guide to Irish Birds*. Mercier Press (Cork, 1967)

Pilcher, J. & Hall, V. *Flora Hibernica*. The Collins Press (Cork, 2001)

Snow, B. & D. *Birds and Berries*. T. & A.D. Poyser (Carlton, 1988)

Svensson, L., Mullarney, K. & Zetterstrom, D. *Collins Bird Guide*. Collins (London, 2000)

An Roinn Oideachais, *Ainmeacha Plandaí agus Ainmhithe*. Department of Education (Dublin, 1978)

Ruttledge, R.F. *A List of the Birds of Ireland*. Stationery Office (Dublin, 1975)

Sample, G. *Bird Songs and Calls of Britain and Northern Europe*. Collins (London, 1996)

Soper, T. *The Bird Table Book*. David & Charles (London, 1986, fifth edition)

Stocker, L. *Saint Tiggywinkle's Wildcare Handbook*. Chatto and Windus (London, 1992)

Various editors, *Irish Birds 1977–1993*. Irish Wildbird Conservancy/Bird-Watch Ireland (Dublin)

Website Resources

www.antaisce.ie
www.biodiversityireland.ie
www.biology.ie
www.birdfood.ie
www.birdlife.org
www.birdwatchgalway.org (BirdWatch Ireland Galway Branch)
www.birdwatchireland.ie
www.birdwatchmayo.org (BirdWatch Ireland Mayo Branch)
www.birdwatchtipp.com (BirdWatch Ireland Tipperary Branch)
www.birdweb.net (BirdWatch Ireland South Dublin Branch)
www.botanicgardens.ie
www.bto.org.uk (Bird conservation and research organisation)
www.buglife.org.uk
www.bwifingal.ie (BirdWatch Ireland Fingal Branch)
www.clarebirdwatching.com (BirdWatch Ireland Clare Branch)
www.cjwildlife.ie (Wild bird food suppliers)
www.coford.ie (National Council for Forest Research and
    Development)
www.crann.ie (Tree conservation organisation)
www.dnfc.net (Dublin Naturalist's Field Club)
www.dublinbirding.ie (BirdWatch Ireland Tolka Branch)
www.enfo.ie (Information on the environment in Ireland)
www.epa.ie (Environmental Protection Agency)
www.froglife.org
www.gardenorganic.co.uk
www.geneticheritageireland.ie
www.habitas.org.uk/bnfc/ (Belfast Naturalist's Field Club)
www.habitas.org.uk/dragonflyireland
www.heritagecouncil.ie
www.heritageknowhow.ie
www.ipcc.ie (Irish Peatland Conservation Council)
www.irishgardenbirds.ie
www.irishseedsavers.ie
www.iwt.ie
www.invasivespeciesireland.com
www.michaelfinnphotography.com
www.mothsireland.com
www.noticenature.ie
www.npws.ie (National Parks and Wildlife Service)
www.organicguide.ie
www.plantlife.org.uk
www.rhs.org.uk (Royal Horticultural Society)
www.rspb.org.uk (Royal Society for the Protection of Birds)

www.rte.ie/mooney
www.sligobirding.com (BirdWatch Ireland Sligo Branch)
www.sonairte.org
www.theorganiccentre.ie
www.treecouncil.ie
www.waterfordbirds.com
www.westcorkbirdwatch.zoomshare.com (BirdWatch Ireland
    West Cork Branch)
www.wcwc.ie (West Clare Wildlife Club)
www.wexfordnaturalists.com
www.wildflowers.ie
www.wildlifetrusts.org
www.woodlandsofireland.com

Photo Credits

All images by Mark Carmody (www.markcarmodyphotography.com), except for the following:

Part I

p. 9 Blue Tit: Oran O'Sullivan (henceforward OOS)

p.10 Mixed Borders: OOS

p.11 Great Tit: OOS

p. 12 Fieldfare: Richard Coombes

p. 13 Peacock butterfly: OOS

p. 15 *Pulmonaria:* OOS; Japanese knotweed: www.biochange.ie

p. 17 Willow Warbler: OOS

p. 18 herbaceous border: OOS; Willow and Alder catkins (OOS)

p. 19 Guelder Rose: OOS

p. 21 mixed herb garden: OOS; Mint: OOS

p. 22 song thrush: OOS

p. 23 sika deer: OOS; vegetable plot: OOS

p. 25 Emperor dragonfly: Michael O'Donnell; garden pond: Jim Wilson

p. 26 frogs: Michael O'Donnell

p. 27 compost bin: OOS

p. 28 water butt: Paula Elmore

p. 30 Blackcaps: Jerry Cassidy

p. 31 Blackthorn: OOS

p. 32 Starling: OOS

p. 33 Spotted Flycatcher: OOS

p. 34 bee in Geranium: OOS

p. 35 House Sparrow: John Carey

p. 36 Blackbird: OOS; Goldenrod: OOS

p. 37 Silver-washed Fritillary: OOS; Red Admiral on Teasel: OOS

p. 38 Redwing: Jim Wilson

p. 39 Bird Table: www.birdfood.ie; Robin in winter: OOS

p. 40 Jay: OOS

p. 41 Siskins: OOS

p. 42 seed mix: OOS; Great Spotted Woodpecker: OOS

p. 45 open-fronted nest box: www.birdfood.ie

p. 47 House Sparrow nest box: www.birdfood.ie

p. 49 Unwelcome visitor: Ronan Browne

p. 50 removing old nest: Jim Wilson

p. 52 'Leave me alone': Jim Wilson

Part 2

Index

Page numbers in bold refer to photographs